Straight
from a
Widow's
Heart

Straight
from a
Widow's
Heart

CANDID CONVERSATIONS
ON LOVE, LOSS, AND
LIVING ON...

MILDRED E. KRENTEL

Faithful Woman® is an imprint of
Cook Communications Ministries, Colorado Springs, CO 80918
Cook Communications, Paris, Ontario
Kingsway Communications, Eastbourne, England

STRAIGHT FROM A WIDOW'S HEART

First printing, 2003
Printed in the United States of America
1 2 3 4 5 6 7 8 9 10 Printing/Year 06 05 04 03

Senior Editor: Janet L. Lee
Editor: Afton Rorvik
Cover and Interior Design: Andrea L. Boven, Boven Design Studio Inc.

Library of Congress Cataloging-in-Publication Data application submitted.

CONTENTS

PREFACE

*T*he legacy of Melmark began with Martha and Melissa Krentel, our daughters. Martha, though born healthy, died suddenly at six months. Such devastation was followed by the arrival of Melissa, born with Down's syndrome. To Paul and me, these events, first grieved, then accepted, became an opportunity: a life's mission.

It took a heartache, the dynamics of a dream, and the unmistakable hand of God to produce Melmark—**Mel** (from Melissa) **mar** (from Martha) and **k** (from Krentel).

We sold our home, raised money by writing letters that shared our dream and took in three other babies with Down's syndrome. A brief year and a half later, with the financial help of many, we moved into a 35-room mansion in Berwyn, Pennsylvania. The year was 1965.

Melmark's initial mission was to provide a safe and nurturing home for Melissa and her friends with similar disabilities. Soon, however, Melmark began to serve children and young adults with increasing levels of disability, meeting educational as well as medical, nursing, and therapeutic needs.

Nestled into a neighborhood of like properties, Melmark's eighty-acre campus now provides its 180 residents a variety of horticultural activities, a barn full of animals, and plenty of open space to enjoy walking, biking, and nature hikes. Melmark School serves children and adolescents with the medical complexities and challenges of mental retardation, autism, and brain injures. Many of our residents live in individual houses, each with its own address and front and back yards in nearby communities.

Our Melissa, now an active thirty-eight year-old woman, enjoys a full life at Melmark.

In 1990 Paul resigned as CEO and president of Melmark, the same year he was diagnosed with Alzheimer's complicated by Parkinson's disease. With the loving help of many caretakers, Paul was able to remained at home. On November 11, 1996, Paul died peacefully in my arms and I began an unexpected journey. I became a widow.

Within the pages that follow I have unzipped my soul, recounting the highs and lows of this journey. It hasn't been easy. I have often wondered why God didn't allow me to leave this earth with Paul. I stumble badly, up one day and down the next. As you read these words, I hope that you will see what God can do with poor material. Think what He can do for you!

Mildred Krentel

A portion of the proceeds from the sale of this book will go to the boys and girls at Melmark.

My dearest Paul,

You have only been gone a few weeks now, but a vast nothingness still permeates our home. That scooped-out place in our king-sized bed where you sprawled next to me is now a forlorn white valley. Your empty lounge chair is a stinging rebuke.

How often I wish you were here with me to talk over things. But that is not to be. So, at the last, there is just this. I will use my computer to write you a message from my throbbing heart.

You must have heard me cry out for you. I was big-time upset with you for leaving me behind. We had done everything together. Why couldn't you have waited for me? Was there no extra room in your golden chariot? You know something? As you lay there dying in my arms, I kept looking for it. Was it there and I just couldn't see it?

But this was your journey, not mine. I had not been invited to go, and so you left me here ... alone.

I have a new name. Widow.

I roll that name around on my tongue to see how it sounds, but I simply don't like the word . . . not one bit.

Honey, you would laugh over the ideas proposed to me "now that I'm a widow." People seem to have forgotten how to comfort. Instead, they are all busy writing out prescriptions for my happiness.

"Why not enroll in college?" They must be kidding! I was never happier than when I said good-bye to my studies.

"Have you thought about taking dancing lessons?" *Why? Who would I dance with? Some bearded old man with bad breath and nothing much to say?*

"Now would be a great time to travel." *But where? And with whom and why? And who would pay the bill?*

The days slowly get easier, but when the sun goes down and the earth gets dark, I still listen for your footsteps. All is silent. There is nobody to cook for, nobody's cheery, "Hi, Honey," simply no reason even to turn on the lights. You are never coming home again. This is such an empty-hammock feeling.

Dinner is something else. Ever heard of cooking for just one—for someone who's not even hungry? So, back to the peanut butter sandwiches. Sometimes I feel like eating a whole can of fruit cocktail. Right out of the can.

My diet is about as lopsided as my body. I am getting plumper. Have you noticed? And I am properly ashamed of myself. So, here I am, virtually as you left me—out of love, out of synch with the rest of the world who sometimes looks at me as though I am some kind of saint just for getting dressed every day and showing up at church on Sunday. Good grief!

I often think about Job and the mess he was in and how his friends wanted nothing more than to accuse him and argue with him. I love it when Job says, "Miserable comforters are you all."

You know what I want? A strong shoulder and a voice that whispers, "I know how hurting you are, Miggy. I'm so sorry. I will pray." Period! End of sentence. And then I want that person to go away and let me sort through my panoply of emotions and ideas. Just me and God.

Guess what song causes me a major meltdown? "I Will Always Love You." Remember? Whitney Houston really knows how to make that song soar. I shamelessly play it as loud as I can tolerate until I hurt and hurt. Then, just when I think I can't stand it one minute longer, I scoop up Melissa, our precious Down's Syndrome daughter, and we 'dance' cheek to cheek, hot tears gluing our faces together until we both collapse in grief.

But I'm not dead yet and God must have some strange reason for leaving me here. So, right now, that's what I must do—find out why! I'll eat up all the casseroles and button up my ears to everybody but God.

Tell God I love Him. If it weren't for Him, I wouldn't stay in this big old house one more night. I wish you could write to me. I miss you so!

Your Miggy

Without your wounds where would your power be? It is your melancholy that makes your low voice tremble into the hearts of men and women. The very angels themselves cannot persuade the wretched and blundering children on earth as can one human being broken on the wheels of living. In Love's service, only wounded soldiers can serve.

—THORNTON WILDER,
THE ANGLE THAT TROUBLED THE WATERS AND OTHER PLAYS

(NEW YORK: COWARD-MCCANN, 1928), P.20.

CHAPTER ONE

Where in the World Are You?

I t was such a small thing, Paul scarcely gave it thought. Nor did I.

"Honey, I can't sign my name anymore. My handwriting gets smaller and smaller. I don't even know what I'm writing." He looked to me for an explanation.

"And you had such great penmanship," I murmured, frowning a bit. "Maybe you need to exercise your hand muscles . . ."

We laughed together and that was that. Strangely enough though, we remembered it the next time Paul was in for a checkup. The doctor thoughtfully scanned the records, as doctors do to give them an extra minute or two, and suggested we see a neurologist.

Two weeks later we were in the neurologist's office talking about some of the little vagaries we had noticed. Paul's voice had lost some of its timbre. Its softness scarcely matched his six feet two inches. Did any of this stuff mean anything?

Turned out it did.

Paul had two out of three early signs of Parkinson's disease. Kind of a litmus test. A shiver went down my spine. What I knew about this disease was precious little. Paul looked as bewildered as I was. We finally went home with two prescriptions in our pockets and a sample of Sinemet in my pocketbook. The year was 1988.

Then all those little things began to snowball. It became increasingly hard for Paul to fit the key in the lock or to pick the right floor on the elevator. No matter what it was, it was the fault of some piece of "inferior equipment." A mysterious someone had messed with it so it no longer functioned. That always infuriated him. Along with the insidious ravages of Parkinson's, Paul's impatience with life in general grew at an alarming rate.

Little did we dream what would unfold in 1990.

Paul had a 1:00 appointment with a doctor in Philadelphia. We were on time and the doctor was prompt—two minor miracles!

Paul had no difficulty talking to the doctor. He was coherent, verbose, and bluntly honest. Tapping his fingers, lifting his feet, he sailed through the little routine tests that signify something meaningful to the neurologist. I sat and listened. I began to wonder what we were doing there.

Back in the car, the scenario changed.

"Turn here. No. Not that way. Here!" I knew it was the wrong way. Finally, I muttered more to myself than to Paul, "Okay, if that's the way you want it, that's the way we'll go!"

We lurched on, right in the thickest of traffic, right into

the middle of the city. We found the Schulykill Expressway, and we rode on in silence. My attitude was not good. Suddenly Paul gestured again and shouted, "Turn right. Turn OFF!"

The sign said, "Lincoln Drive, Route 3." Paul became increasingly agitated, so I turned. Twenty minutes later, we were in Mount Airy, a place I knew nothing about. I turned around in a gas station and headed the other way.

Neither one of us said a thing. I prayed silently and tried to make meaningless chatter to defuse the tense situation.

Even though Paul admitted his driving skills had changed *(only slightly, mind you)*, he handed over the car keys with barely concealed resentment. And only after the urging of our regular doctor.

"I suppose you think you're great now that you have the wheel. You have all the power I used to have."

Paul's words crushed me though I knew in my heart he did not mean them.

Parkinson's clearly was now courting another companion within Paul's body. I dreaded it with every fiber of my being. Nobody had to tell me the name or the symptoms of this companion. I knew its name and recognized its symptoms. I could almost see Paul's mind crumbling. Every day another chunk of it crashed to the earth. That killer disease— Alzheimer's.

And then we flew down for a holiday in Florida. One morning, I scribbled this in my journal:

Today is a moody day. Clouds, rain, fog ... wind—all taking turns. Paul is napping. But I hesitate to write. I feel as though I can't trust my pen. It might betray me, and I would be entangled forever in a web of my own making. Maybe I don't trust myself. If I don't put it into words, then clearly it isn't really here—it's gone forever. I feel trapped today. There is no escape from reality and the truth is very heavy. The telephone does not ring. I'm lonely and most of all, I need a hug. I miss you, Honey.

Several days later we drove in torrential rain and tortuous traffic to finish a few errands. Stopping at Ritz Camera, we picked up our photos. Each picture was double-exposed. Paul was depressed, and I, as usual, probed as to why he rewound the film. He retreated into silence. We walked through the sunshine (which only Florida can produce in a wink) and, on the way home, we made a stop at the Publix market. Paul stayed in the car.

Mission accomplished, we headed home. I spoke carefully. "Honey, I know we are both going through our own private world of torment. No, please let me finish. I don't know how we will make it, but remember I love you."

We kissed all the way up in the elevator. When we closed the door to our condominium, we clung to one another. Then Paul shared his confusion, admitting that his inability to perform certain tasks caused him great emotional stress. His biggest hurdle was handing the car keys over to me. Putting the house keys in the lock also troubled him. His fingers did not work the way they used to, yet he was stubborn enough to hang on to his few responsibilities.

George Beverly Shea came on the radio just then with his booming voice, reminding me, "God will take care of you."

Will You really, God? Why can't I trust You more? Do I think by my own incessant griping and pointing out what I presume to be great dangers that I hold it in my power to provide safety for us? Are You sufficient God? What should I do? God, will You help me?

It became definite. Paul had a dual diagnosis: Alzheimer's and Parkinson's! An interesting pair. What one doesn't do, the other will. Yet just when I was convinced Paul was on a slippery slide, he would do a right about-face and say things that made me wonder. To be brutally honest, however, those days became more and more rare.

Soon Paul needed help dressing, shaving, and showering. His aphasia continued to greatly distress him. He couldn't find the correct names for the most simple, everyday objects.

I found myself living with a man who looked like Paul and sounded like Paul, but my real Paul was no longer present. It was like having a death in the family without benefit of a funeral. Paul's body is still here.

Aggravating? Tremendously! Frustrating—almost always. Heartbreaking? It shattered me.

He tried and tried to accomplish the simplest of tasks by himself. Sometimes he succeeded and sometimes not.

I must share these thoughts, written by someone who

had Alzheimer's and recorded in the book *The Loss of Self,* written by Donna Cohen, Ph.D. and Carl Eisdorfer, Ph.D., M.D. (New York: New American Library, 1986, p. 22).

> No theory of medicine can explain what is happening to me. Every few months I sense that another piece of me is missing. My life—myself—are falling apart. I can only think half-thoughts now. Someday I may wake up and not think at all—not know who I am. Most people expect to die someday, but whoever expects to lose their self first?

Alzheimer's is a cruel disorder. The death of the mind is the worst death imaginable and to witness the disintegration of someone you love right before your very eyes is frightening.

Strangely enough Paul and I could still laugh together. We decided we must do this or we would surely cry until our tears ran dry. And so, as Paul stood behind me, trying to master the mystery of buttoning up his pants and making his belt behave, we laughed.

I have heard the phrase that God goes before you. I believe it. I had not even dared to pray for someone to relieve me. But God decided I needed help. And He went before me. Her name was Diane. She was a Philadelphia College of the Bible graduate with the disposition of a saint.

I was so nervous. I knew I would babble like a fool, not knowing what to ask her to do. How could I ever get myself organized?

Even at the end of the seventh week, I kept waiting for

the honeymoon to peter out, but it didn't. Diane worked from Monday morning until Friday night. Her great sense of humor, laced with a most gentle spirit, wore well. Paul liked her immediately. As for me, it was so wonderful to have an adult to talk to, to share "girl" things with and sometimes just to cry with.

God is so good.

CHAPTER TWO

The Yo-Yo Days

*I*t was on a beautiful Palm Sunday when I discovered that I could well have been numbered with those who spread their garments of praise one moment and shouted, "Crucify Him!" with the next breath.

My cup ran over, and I spilled out what must have been dammed up for awhile. Paul and I had a full-blown quarrel. I do not even remember who lit the match. Is it ever worth remembering?

Paul was angry and extremely coherent as we argued. Back and forth it went. I marveled how Paul could gather his thoughts so coherently to strike back at me when often he could not even finish one complete sentence.

"Sometimes it seems as though you are okay, so I must be the sick one." I blurted it out—shamelessly.

I crushed him. I ignored God's checking (that inner voice). I was driven by anger ... resentment ... confusion.

Oh, I even enjoyed it. Center stage for me. I slammed

the door, threatened to leave forever, and protested my innocence. But Paul wasn't buying. And he was right. I was wrong.

Dear God, have You turned away from me?

That night there was an ear-splitting thunderstorm, and we crawled into our big king-sized bed together. I took his face in my hands and said, "Paul, I will never ever do that again to you. I am flattened. I have been saturated with self and the picture is devastating. I despair of who I am, but I promise you, I will never ever do that again to you. I can only ask you to forgive me."

Paul's eyes filled with tears. He protested against the extravagance of my confession and held me in his arms. I did not deserve it. I woke up the next morning, still filled with remorse, confessing again to God and asking Him for new strength—just for the day.

I did not understand life. Why did I cry every morning? Where had all my laughter gone? Bring on the clowns!

I will never understand how God manages it, but each new day with Him is exactly that—brand-new! Why did I forget so easily?

Back home again in Pennsylvania, we picked up the threads of our family life. Paul slipped into a confused state. One moment with us, and the next in a make-believe world of his own making.

I found myself often upset with Paul. My mind told me he could not help the things he did or said, but my heart hurt. My soul was smitten. Had he forgotten how we fell in love in college and married the end of his junior year?

Married life had seemed to me an unending slumber party with my best friend. And now, this man that I had loved so long was unreasonable, demanding, and sublimely selfish. Here we were. Drowning in this dreadful disease. This was not my Paul. And I grieved for what he was.

Dear God, what can I do to recapture our love? Will it ever be the same? Has he changed forever now? Then, please help me recognize that this is my reality and that there is no looking back or yearning for things as they were. Give me Your calm and a quiet heart, one that does not react, but quite independent of external causes, is at peace. I long to be unruffled and not to act unbecomingly.

I already know Your answer. There is only one—stay close to You. God is the Fountain Head. So again, day after day, I come.

Do You ever tire of seeing me, God?
Please, God. I want You to be at home in my heart.
God, forgive me—I am not skilled to understand. I do know when all is not right in my heart, and I do run to You—but not quickly enough. Am I just seeking your goodies? Your gifts? Forgive me for asking for wrong things. Wash me clean, be my strength, my compassion, my life. Live it for me. I am no longer able to. I cannot sort out the intricate weavings, the tangled threads of my life. I never know what You are doing.

"Let us then approach the throne of grace with confidence,
so that we may receive mercy and find grace to help us
in our time of need" (Hebrews 4:16).

Then came another day. Thursday. It seemed to have no special reason for being—yet here it was. I barely greeted it. How could I stand to live one more day? What should I do with all those hours? Wash the dishes, make the beds, dust the house and wash the clothes—everyday dumb stuff! And dear Paul, my husband of fifty-five years, sat in his chair, getting no better, moaning constantly.

"What's bothering you, Honey?"

"My feet. My feet. They're hurting."

I found a tin tub out in the garage and filled it with warm water. Then I sprinkled in an envelope of Dr. Scholl's comfort-soak powder. Paul plunked his big feet into the water. Miracle of miracles—they fit.

Paul's feet had been cramping one moment, paining the next and finally going into painful spasms. I had tried everything to relieve it. This was just one in our list of solutions.

After he soaked his feet for fifteen minutes, I sat on the floor and dried them with a big bath towel. Rubbing a mentholated cream on his heels, his arches and then his toes, I slowly massaged his feet in my hands. A peaceful look came over his face as he looked at me. He was visibly touched by the whole procedure.

I thought about Jesus washing His disciples' feet. It was indeed a lowly task. Perhaps that was why He had admonished us to wash one another's feet. He knew that it was difficult for us to humble ourselves.

Feet are not the most attractive part of our bodies, let's face it.

There is no room for pride or puffiness when you lift another's foot, take it in both your hands and slowly massage the aching muscles.

It is probably the reason Jesus loved Mary sitting at His feet to hear more about His life and His plan. Just a little bit away, Martha stood on her own two tired feet in the kitchen, scrubbing the potatoes. I well imagine her feet ached and that she would have welcomed someone tenderly offering to wash her feet. But she was using her feet to do what Jesus needed at this moment.

Dear God, whatever You have planned for today, prepare me. If it is the bucket of water, make it healing. If my words, make them shine. Or, if You just want me to sit at Your feet to learn of You, settle me down and help me take these moments to listen.

The next morning I was awakened by someone standing by my side of the king-sized bed. It was our daughter, Melissa. I had learned that if I did not open my eyes, she would bend over and kiss me. I had one of two options—move over or get up and make the coffee.

Groggy with sleep, Melissa and I went out to the kitchen to make Paul's favorite brew. Melissa pulled out our largest tray and spread a clean kitchen towel on it, took three napkins and folded them carefully and then added three mugs. She had remembered our age-old custom of Saturday mornings together in the big bed, watching cartoons with Daddy and Mommy.

But life was different now. Daddy had changed.

We turned and there he was, watching us—no smile—just one question he kept repeating over and over: "Where are my pills?"

They were there on the tray with a glass of water. He picked up the glass in one hand and the pill in the other. First he raised his right hand, then stopped and raised his left hand. He could not make up his mind what came first—the pills or the water. My heart plummeted.

I poured the coffee, added cream, and we three stood there. Solemnly we raised our mugs, touched rims and mouthed the heartrending toast "Cheers!".

Paul put his arms around the two of us and we stood there, close together—hugging. We were still a family.

Even though it was only two years since his Alzheimer's diagnosis, Paul had spiraled downwards until his debilitating disease dictated my entire life. When some of my acquaintances marveled that I kept him at home, I wanted to ask them one question: "What did you think it meant when you exchanged vows—for better or worse?" Sure this was worse, but so what? Did that make the vow less binding?

When I peeled away his confusion, scraped off his aphasia, I could still find that layer of the love that had kept us together for the last fifty-five years.

I'll never forget when Paul told me that he thought it

was about time.

"Time for what?"

"Time for me to tell my wife about you."

I smiled at him through my tears.

CHAPTER THREE

Yesterday's Prayers and Leftover Blessings

*D*ay followed day, each with its own despair. Paul was on a roller coaster, gliding from cognizance to never-never land. His mouth was full of words. Love words, unfamiliar cursing. He lived in a room peopled with dead babies whom he reached for vainly with groping fingers, leaning forward in his chair, his eyes vacant yet occupied with his inner world. Intrigued by his personal nightmares.

Paul seemed to pass from one stage to the other seamlessly. Each one was a bit worse than the last. He lost the ability to say or do even the little things. Sometimes I could hardly catch my breath watching the rapidity with which he slid— always downwards.

I remember one family supper. Meat loaf, mashed potatoes and the required veggies. Paul was in his wheelchair with Derrick, his caregiver, by his side. And eldest son, David, seated by Melissa.

Paul, intent on his own small hill of mashed potatoes,

made a sloppy valley in the middle with his fist. After licking his fingers clean, he looked around, then stared at the ceiling. After what seemed the longest while, he started reaching for something. Over and over, his big hand stretched to grasp at the air, his fingers opening and closing. Even Melissa watched him.

David, always interested in what motivated his dad to do certain things, asked him, "What is it, Dad? What do you see?"

"Don't you see it up there?" Paul responded with irritation. "It's blue and yellow and there's a green one too."

Now he had us all mesmerized. We looked, in spite of ourselves, with small smiles hesitating at the corners of our mouths. Melissa, too, watched with fascination.

Suddenly she stood to her feet and walked over to Paul.

"That's mine!" she declared, ownership oozing out of every pore. "The passing of the spirit of heaviness."

I wrote in my journal that evening.

Perhaps those who see me look for tears, signs of weeping in the night, desolation in the daylight hours … but they have passed for the moment and shall I not praise Him? Shall I refrain from putting on the "garment of praise" lest my desolation returns? Shall I set a watch looking for my familiar bedfellows to come a-knocking? No. I will bolt the door, knowing full well the vagaries of life … the often transitory nature of happiness. I will not succumb to the wiles of the evil one. I will run to my High Tower and shut the door. Then I will be safe.

"The name of the LORD is a strong tower; the righteous run to it and are safe" (Proverbs 18:10).

But all things remained the same. The vial of troubles had not been emptied. There seemed to be no light on the horizon, no dawning of a new day. Yet I vowed to live out those moments allotted to me and welcome what God permitted.

I did not like His diet, but I loved what it accomplished in my life.

Paul's perspective on life often came out in his prayers and frequent off-the-wall comments. I knew his faith in God was complete, his trust childlike. In his prayers even his love for me came poking through at the oddest moments.

"Thank You, Father, for the rain and those who were responsible for it."

And who among us could possibly sneeze like a gigantic explosion and then yell at the top of his lungs, "NEXT!"

And then the comment that sent his caregiver and me sinking to the floor in hysteria one morning ... an innocent remark made when we were changing him.

He looked at us and said, "Uh-oh!"

Instantly I said, "What?" fearing the worst.

"I think I just made an artificial fartle." There was nothing artificial about the new aroma in his bedroom.

I'll never forget the prayer he made one day while contentedly petting our obedient collie.

"God we just want to thank You for all our blessings . . ."

Here he paused.

"Minus one or two things." Then he stopped, for he heard my stuffed laughter.

He was right of course. Behind his confusion, out of sight and hard to find, somewhere were all the qualities that made me fall in love with him. I still saw glimpses of them.

Scripture was hopelessly garbled in his mind.

"The Lord is NOT my shepherd, I shall not want. He makes me lie down in a … jug!" I never corrected him. God knew what he meant. But every now and again, I completely lost my perspective and found myself reacting to what my ears heard. I was wrong—dead wrong! And guiltily, I knew in my inner core that most of the trouble was with me.

Paul called out to me frequently: "Mom … Mother!" I answered. The fact that he did not respond is of little moment. He knew I was there.

I still teased him and acted foolish until I could find his lopsided grin. Pecks on his neck, his eyes and his cheeks. He drank it in like a thirsty camel.

By this time, our family of caregivers had grown. When Paul insisted on mixing up his days and nights, we had a jolly good time patching our schedules together.

We had started with Diane, but now that she had left to be a missionary in Russia, we added an older man, a recovered alcoholic, who viewed his life as a ministry to others. John was a respected worker at Melmark, the residential home that we establish with God's help after the birth of our Down's syndrome daughter, Melissa.

He amazed me every time I saw him. Nothing was too lowly for him to do. No service too demanding, no call to duty he would not answer. How God blessed me in providing this kind of "stand-by-me" caregiver was nothing short of miraculous. God found them, God hired them and God kept them.

And, in so doing, God kept me.

When his nighttime wanderings became his second career, and acting as a professional mover—a third, we moved Paul to a spare bedroom so that I could get enough sleep to equip me for my daytime responsibility of caring for my honey. A hospital bed also became a welcome addition, keeping Paul from falling and hurting himself.

One morning I heard the sounds of Paul coming over the nursery monitor which was right by my bedside. Lying in his hospital bed, mouth open, regular rhythmic snoring. Suddenly a gentle voice whispered, "Good morning." Then a long pause. "Good morning Mr. K." It was John.

The sound of the radio in the background—"Have thine own way, Lord"—then the opening of the Venetian blinds and the rattle of the sides of the hospital bed crashing down. I lay there in bed listening, identifying each sound. Then I heard John praying:

"Dear Father, thank You for giving us such a nice day. Thank You for the sunshine. Thank You for the night's rest. Now help us this day in Your service to do whatever You have for us to do. In Jesus' name, Amen."

John's voice was steady and sure.

"Good morning, Mr. K. We are going to get up now and have a sponge bath instead of a shower. How about it?"

As I listened, I prayed to God just to get us through one more day. My prayers were usually like bullets zinging toward Heaven. But this morning, I just took my time. God was the faithful One—always there. And He listened while I babbled on. It seemed I flitted from one crisis to another. God never gave me enough peace to hoard for the next emergency. I think He liked it that way—cause then I had to keep coming to Him over and over. It was kind of like the manna in the Old Testament that got stale if the Israelites tried to save it for the next day. Just take enough for the day.

And I did. That way I didn't forget where it came from or how badly I needed it. If I tried to make it on my own on yesterday's prayers and leftover blessings—I crashed. Flat out!

Dear God, I am totally afraid of the future. All I can see down the road is sadness, dissolution of relationships, agony of soul, and a too-long life when nothing would suit me better than to lay me down to sleep and wake up in Heaven. God listen, please! Let me live long enough to watch over Paul until You call him and then, call me swiftly please. To watch him break apart, piece by piece, is breaking my heart. Help me!

CHAPTER FOUR

It Happened on Monday

I never could have endured the unpredictability of life with Paul without outside help. But God knew my need was escalating, and He had gone ahead and set apart three young university students whom I soon grew to love and lean on. Two were from Kenya and one from Uganda. They were my three "other" sons—John, George, and Derreck. They gobbled up all the work they could find to help pay their school tuition.

The first day that John came, Paul looked at him, filled the bellows of both lungs and yelled, "Murder, Mother! Murder!!!"

But John was not one to frighten off that easily. He stayed on. Too soon, the day arrived that I had to ask him, "John, do you know anybody else that could help us out? The other John is on a special project for Melmark and without him, we're going under."

"I have an older brother, George," he offered.

"Is he as good as you are?"

"Better," he said. "I'll speak to him and see what time he can give us."

It was always "us." We filled up the gaps in each other's schedules and somehow John assumed the role of head scheduler—always faithful, showing up day after day on time.

His brother, George, was just as wonderful, with a deep baritone voice that got a daily airing when he sang to Paul the hymns he knew and loved. And soon Paul's uncertain tenor would join in, trying to find the tune.

Derreck was, well, he was just Derreck. Tall, skinny, always trying to find the right gal, charming everyone within hearing distance with his gift of gab.

Together, they gave me life when there was none to be had. They made me laugh when nothing was funny. They hugged me when Paul would have none of me. They even praised me for my fallen pound cake running all over the oven but, of course, they soon learned to make it themselves. They were priceless.

Paul knew it too. Soon I found him groping for their brown-skinned hands rather than my speckled white ones. I could not blame him. They stuck by us through thick and thin.

Four long years of day-after-day living passed this way. Years that promised little hope, but held much in the tears and exasperation department. Paul's days and nights were all different—funny, strange and confusing. They clustered together into months and fashioned into years, they all passed by. I was happy to see them go and weary of greeting another day.

Then the Sunday morning before Veteran's Day 1996, I heard Paul call out for me. It was a loud outcry of distress. I ran. His eyes were sunken circles of fear. He shivered and shook almost uncontrollably.

"Hold me! Hold me!" his words were urgent. I wrapped my whole self around him and held him … tightly. Cradling his head in my arms, I nuzzled my face in his neck. I knew something unusual was happening to my dear one. He had gone through so much suffering. Two broken hips, eight years of Parkinson's coupled with six years battling that killer disease, Alzheimer's.

He never ate that Sunday except for his pills, disguised in applesauce and sugar. But he did sleep. All that day and all night long. We stood by and watched.

When I peeked into Paul's bedroom the next morning, my mug of coffee in my hand, his eyes were tightly closed. Almost as though he were wishing himself out of his hospital bed, away from this humiliating situation, or just plain "outta here" as my grandsons would say. Why did I sense somehow that today my life would change?

He just lay there in his hospital bed. I talked to him softly, but there was no response. Opening the window to freshen up his room, I prayed John would soon get there. When he arrived, we spoke in hushed tones.

"John, let's sponge bathe him this morning in his bed. I think he is too weak to have a shower."

John never disagreed but always did what he thought was

best in a way that never seemed to contradict what I said.

"Mum, he will feel a whole lot better if we shower him."
So, together we bundled him up in his wheelchair and
wheeled him into the bathroom. Holding his head close
while the water sprinkled on both of us, I gently shampooed
his white hair.

"Are you hurting, Honey?"

But he had no words. He slumped into a forlorn heap
much like a rag doll. We finished quickly and he sat in his
chair leaning hard against me while John changed his bed. The
sweet smell of Johnson's baby powder overcame all else and
soon he was back in bed in his blue pajamas. Tentatively, he
stretched his long legs.

"Look at him, Mum. He feels a whole sight better."

But Paul turned away the spoonful of oatmeal and refused
to open his mouth, even for coffee. His eyes were squeezed
shut. Almost as though he were willing everyone to disappear.
Me included!

The minutes ticked away as we waited for the nurse. His
forehead felt hotter than usual, but with me ready to fly into
a panic attack, I was not a good judge. The familiar hum of
the washing machine and the chimes of the grandfather's
clock in the background all worked together, trying hard to
change this day into a normal Monday morning. But my
sense of foreboding remained.

I don't remember praying. It seemed I was suspended . . .
watching what was happening and waiting. My life was
unraveling steadily. I sat by Paul's bed, listening to him moan.
Then I stood and, leaning over, cradled his head in my arms.

Carmen, the community nurse, arrived, took Paul's temperature and then disappeared into my office. I heard her on the phone. I heard the word *hospice*. A shiver went from my head to my toes. I stroked Paul's head gently and bent over to catch the rhythm of his breathing. His breaths were becoming shallower and shallower.

"Are you dying, my beloved? Is God getting ready to take you home now? Can you hear me, Paul? You are going on ahead of me, aren't you? We always did everything together. Why, oh why, can't I go too? Honey, you are gently slipping away from me and my heart is going with you. I do not think I can handle it."

I called for John to get the nurse. They both came running and stood there with me. There were no angels, just the faint sound of Paul's last breath. And then he was gone. Just like that—no gasping, no frightening rattle—just an emptiness. Suddenly I was alone. I kissed Paul's face and the top of his head until the warmth drained and the coldness of death took over. Still I could not leave. But I knew I must call our children.

David and Steve came over almost immediately, but Bob was on the West Coast. He would be here as soon as he could. Diane, our daughter, lived over four hours away in Albany, New York. She literally came apart at the seams when I told her. She had always been "Daddy's girl."

"I'm coming, Mom. I wanted so much to be there with him. I never even got to say goodbye." It was all she could manage through her tears.

So I simply shut the door to his bedroom. One by one the

family assembled and we put the bits and pieces of our daily living together so we could tackle the bigger issues. There's a lot to handle when a loved one dies—plans for the funeral and burial and all those demanding things that intrude on the moment.

Before the day was done, each family member in his own way took the time to go inside Paul's bedroom to say their good byes—without fanfare, without an audience.

Monday. Veteran's Day! The day my hero left this earth.

CHAPTER FIVE

"It Won't Rain Always"

*M*usic has always played a major role in my life. It was no different when Paul's funeral was over. Time had been suspended. Now I had to learn how to live all over again. A life without Paul. There were so many daily things to deal with. Bills, letters, notifying all the right people. Could I do it all?

I turned on one of my favorite CDs and listened carefully. Bill Gaither has always been one of my favorites, and the lyrics of this song burned themselves into my soul. I played it over and over, crying inside and outside. Sometimes you just have to weep to wear down the sharp contours of grief. And it is okay, no matter what the skeptics say.

The hurt can't hurt forever and the tears are sure to dry,
and it won't rain always, the clouds will soon be gone.
The sun's gonna shine in God's own good time, and He
will see you through.

I let this truth sink into my being, and I permitted myself to continue weeping. I felt as though I would weep forever.

It was one of those days that I seemed to touch bottom. The house was too quiet. There was just this smothering stillness. It felt as if someone had injected me with a giant dose of Novocain.

I numbly greeted the morning and knew that when the day was finished, I would gratefully accept the darkness. My main trouble was the daytime. I didn't know what to do with myself during the daylight hours. My mind played hopscotch and I could not concentrate.

Our house was crammed with the special things that had provided a support system for Paul's worn-out body. They were sharp stabs of remembering as I passed them. No longer needed.

A brown, headless teddy bear leaned forlornly against Paul's pillow in his barren hospital bed. I remember how Paul had twisted off its sturdy head. I never could discover how to put it back together again. Now it sat, broken and sad, like my hero who had gone on ahead. His Dallas Cowboys hat, tribute to his never dying allegiance to America's Team, was sliding off the bed. It was all so final. Death had come and slammed the door shut smack in my face.

"Don't go in Paul's room," my mind screamed. "It's a whirlpool. You'll get sucked under. No backing up, just keep going forward. Too dangerous for memories right now."

My sobs were more like a groan as the tears spilled down my cheeks.

Dear God, my heart keeps breaking over and over in the same places, and the pieces are so jagged that this time I might not live. The tears I cry are tears I've used before, the agony I feel is strange yet somehow familiar. I see it coming from afar. I wish that I could reach an end to this earthly life. Yet I know that I do not have that privilege. It is my duty to keep on living until You call. I despair at the prospect. God, how long will it be?

One night around midnight, trying to find the blissful anesthesia of sleep, I started to quote all the Scripture I knew in my heart. Of course, I began by reciting the 23rd Psalm: "The Lord is my Shepherd, I shall not want... ." But right there, in the very beginning, I panicked. What came next? Had I forgotten? And then I started all over and stumbled again!

Doesn't everyone know the 23rd Psalm? I thought as I tumbled out of bed and groped my way into my office to find my Bible. The house was cold and black as midnight.

I read that Psalm over and over—a reassurance to hug to my heart. But why had I not even remembered what came next? I felt shamed, rebuked by the Spirit, nakedly aware of what a poor Christian I was. I had a new charge to keep. I must learn these verses by heart so that in my darkest days and nights, I could remember them and pour them like salve over my wounds. God had promised that His Word would not return to Him void.

The LORD is my shepherd, I shall not be in want.
He makes me lie down in green pastures,
he leads me beside quiet waters, he restores my soul.
He guides me in paths of righteousness, for his name's sake.
Even though I walk through the valley of the shadow
of death,
I will fear no evil for you are with me;
your rod and your staff, they comfort me.
You prepare a table before me in the presence of my enemies,
You anoint my head with oil; my cup overflows.
Surely goodness and love will follow me all the days of my life,
and I will dwell in the house of the LORD forever.

I could expect comfort, guidance, and a balm in Gilead. It was there for the asking and I had ignored it. Sure, I had prayed, but I had not listened to God. I had not given Him a chance. For I had neglected reading His love letters to me. With tears streaming down my cheek, I hunched over my desk and touched the pages of my Bible, smoothing each wrinkle, barely able to make out the words through my tears.

And then it was Friday. The weather outside fell short of anybody's definition of a good and proper Friday. It was a strange day. In the morning, despite the sheeting rain, I ventured out to the local supermarket. Completely enmeshed by the ministry of the mundane, I did those daily, tedious things that demand doing.

I practically swam out to the car in the parking lot and cautiously wended my disgruntled way home while Hurricane

Floyd gathered his strength and fury to present himself as a grownup hurricane—which he did by his own timetable. The rain sheeted out of the sky, drenching any and everything.

Once home I was cozy inside and the TV told me in spades what was happening around town. I read and drank hot coffee and washed every little bit of laundry around. I did the dishes and even hard-boiled some eggs, just in case. As long as I was busy, all was fine. The hurricane was a spectator sport. But when the electricity went out, I became the quarterback. I gathered all the large candles I could find before the daylight disappeared and settled down for what I dared to hope was just a short outage. It was 3:45 P.M.

I snacked on peanut butter and cold eggs and a candy bar. Mentally I kept notes for Y2K. What must I have in preparation? A good reading light for sure. For as the daylight faded and the skies were black, the house grew larger and even more lonesome.

Hurricanes never seem to matter when you are with someone you love. Alone, the hours go by slowly.

The trees swayed in the wind, quite majestically really, almost as if to say, "Hey, we have been here too long, and you shall not dislodge us. Our roots are deep, and we have learned to sway and bend to the irrational winds of time. Do your worst, Floyd. We shall ride it out."

And ride it out they did! No matter the weather! Life's storms, unexpected and swift, blast their ferocity around us. Then, and then only, can we know how deep our roots go.

I had a strange new worry, a storm of my own. Since Paul had died, I found that this uninvited fear kept poking its way into my consciousness. The fear that God will let Satan test me in the area of my own personal health. Why did I feel this sense of foreboding? I think I did not trust Him completely. Sometimes, I confess, I lived in my thought world. *What's next, God?* Kind of like waiting for the other shoe to drop. This was not a very trusting relationship to have with my best friend.

Dear God, release me from anticipating what is going to happen around the next bend of the road. The pathway to Heaven is different when you walk alone. I know You understand that. For You even said in Your Bible: "Religion that God our Father accepts as pure and faultless is this: to look after orphans and widows in their distress and to keep oneself from being polluted by the world" (James 1:27). So You must have known that widows get lonely ... and distressed. Not every day, but almost. And on those days, sometimes we can't remember where You are and more importantly Who You are!

Does it cause You great unhappiness? We make the same mistakes over and over. Are we all slow learners?

From the Sublime to the Ridiculous

*A*s I walked by Paul's bedroom door again, I looked in. The headless body of the teddy bear seemed to beckon me, so I picked it up and hugged it to me. Precisely at that moment, the front doorbell rang.

John, still faithful in his helping ministry, had just returned with our two dogs from the vet. I thanked him profusely.

One slightly goofy Great Pyrenees and one getting-older collie. I remember when I first got them. I thought I did it for Paul, but it was really for me.

Oh, indeed, Paul had loved both of them. He let them lick his face, smear his glasses and walk on his tummy. They had even cleaned up the surplus food on his bib.

I remember Paul's prayer one night before supper.

"Now, Lord we know this little thumpkin is a piece of Your creation and we get blessing from it. We could get more … but we don't know how."

I think I can safely say that Princess, the Great Pyrenees,

and I finally bonded. She did, however, win just about every argument we had, including the cage to sleep in at night. I bought her the biggest one I could find to the tune of $200, and she clawed her way through one end, bending and breaking every wire in sight.

Finally I gave in. I had few open options anyway. Princess wanted to sleep on my bedroom floor just like her buddy, Viking. Somehow she knew that was where Viking disappeared every night.

So in she trotted, triumph oozing from every pore. I slept fitfully, for I was sure the room would be in shambles when I awoke. But outside of knocking my comb, brush and mirror off the bureau, she thumped down in front of the open window and slept like a lamb. Both dogs woke me at 6:00 or thereabouts by trying to jump up on my high four-poster bed.

So much for cage training! I returned the shattered cage to the store where the shopkeeper handed me back all my money. I heard him mutter, "I've never seen a cage torn up like this."

I sometimes questioned my sanity as Princess trotted on by me to the back porch with something forbidden in her mouth. Then she skulked behind the table and waited for me to yell, "PRINCESS!!!!" I learned not to chase her, for she always won by running in circles. Unfortunately, it was usually the remote control for the TVs that fascinated her.

But, as a new widow and quite alone, I was so grateful that the dogs were there, for the things that go bump in the night managed to cause me a fright. With Princess I had company at the oddest hours. Who else would sprawl right alongside the bathtub each night, waiting for me patiently while I soaked in my bubble bath? Who else would get up every night with me at three o'clock in the morning and sleepily stumble alongside me to the bathroom? Once there, Princess plopped down in front of me with her big white head drooping in my lap while I scratched her ears. Then together we crept back to the darkened bedroom. Kind of took the edge out of the blackness.

So, all in all it was a delicate balancing act. I came to treasure our relationship in spite of our hide and seek games and the things that were chewed beyond recognition. I tolerated her wicked ways, and she tolerated my inconsistent behavior.

I bathed her in my shower with much yanking and tugging. She emerged looking so beautiful I wanted to freeze dry her. But she could find more mud and dig more holes than I ever thought possible. And her coat was supposed to be snow white! Ludicrous! Outsiders might have deduced that my life had clearly gone to the dogs. I would not dare to argue.

One morning I was so furious with both of them. I was awakened at 3:00 A.M. by Princess stalking up and down in the bedroom and panting heavily. This behavior bore all the signs of an imminent disaster if I did not hop out of bed, disengage the alarm system and let her out in the backyard. But I was loath to leave my warm nest!

So, in my sternest voice, I commanded her to "LIE DOWN!" She obliged that command for the space of two minutes. After which, she resumed her panting and stalking. She was soon joined in her parade by my collie Viking.

I was not convinced that this was anything but a dirty trick. I jumped out of bed and verbally abused them. I informed them of their rights but told them that I had rights also.

I then hit upon a wonderful idea. I separated them and shut Princess up in my bathroom. I knew Viking would behave for he was the perfect gentleman.

Back in bed, I covered up my head and tried to find the dream I had been dreaming. No luck! In another few moments, I heard a loud crash and the sound of broken glass. I dashed into the bathroom and discovered that Princess had taken care of her problem in my sunken bathtub. In catapulting out of the tub, she had broken some of my seashells on the glass shelf.

Now, did I follow through as all good dog owners would? No, I collapsed on the floor with laughter. I could not scold; I thought she was a pretty smart dog.

Since they had so easily won that round, I let them both out in the yard. Whereupon Viking commenced barking at some unseen foe in the woods while I bounced in and out of bed, knocking frantically on the window and screaming at them to STOP barking.

At this point it was clearly a draw, so I let them back in the house. Of course, the minute they came in they turned into doggie angels, sleeping back to back, snorting, and twitching in their doggie nightmares of their cruel mistress.

Sometimes I wonder if God laughs with me over the

dilemmas I get myself into. Seriously, if I were God, I would make it a commandment that all people who live by themselves should find a dog to keep them company. These four-legged animals have more assets than many two-legged specimens.

It gets lonesome in the middle of the dark.

CHAPTER SEVEN

Running Away on Christmas Eve

*E*ver had a restless heart? Oh, it does the job well enough, keeps the red blood flowing, but there is little peace. It thumps out of synch with the rest of your body. One minute you want to run away, stop the world and get off, the next—lie down and cover up your head. Restlessness is contagious, spreads from your heart to your soul.

My restlessness overwhelmed me one day when I heard a plane overhead. I began to dream of flying somewhere— anywhere, just to get away from the daily sameness of life. But when that minute had passed, I knew intuitively that it was time for me to talk to God. I picked up my Bible, read a few verses, then set it aside. I hunted for my daily devotional— perhaps that would steady me. But my gaze jumped off the page and out the window.

The chickadees and finch at the bird feeder were chirping noisily and happily. I gazed at my collie and Great Pyrenees sprawled on the floor side by side, dreaming doggie dreams and shivering with delight. And I wondered!

The whole animal kingdom seems wiser than this soul of mine tossed to and fro. I need an anchor, God, to quiet my soul. But I already have One that keeps me from drifting too far. So then, what is it that prevents me from using my Anchor to settle down in the deep? That's the problem. I am simply not there in the deep, and the waves are more apt to push me around because I am floundering in the shallows.

My second Christmas without Paul was fast approaching. The thought of enduring Christmas again in a memory-packed home frightened me.

The song on the radio promised, "I'll be home for Christmas." I began to cry—just baby tears at first, but soon they threatened to become a veritable downpour. *What was it about that song?* It unzipped me every time I heard it.

Holidays were sad days. Melissa was excited, but all I could think about was what another Christmas would be like without Paul. Last year, my grief was fresh, and I had traveled to Spokane with Melissa to be with my son and his family. But now I was home. I kept Kleenex handy the month of December.

I wished for nothing more than to have my whole family together on holidays, but Melissa's three older brothers and one sister were grown and married and scattered all over the map. They could not always travel to my house for the holidays. They had their own families too.

A little sign hanging over the kitchen sink made me weep every time I spotted it: *Home for Christmas.* So, one day, I yanked it off the nail and threw it in the trash.

"Foolish thing," I muttered "Home for Christmas indeed!"

But Christmas kept right on coming! The radio, TV, and department stores reminded me daily. So, all in secret, I planned to run away on Christmas Eve with Melissa. *Maybe,* I thought to myself, *maybe in another state far, far away, the calendar will just skip over the 25th of December.*

When I telephoned the news to my family, my children were horrified.

"Why would you leave home on Christmas Eve?"

"We never dreamed you'd be away on Christmas Day!"

"You could visit with us, you know."

Yes, I knew. I knew, too, that Melissa would hover on the fringes of all the activities, not because she was not loved or included, but because normal lives moved in fast and complicated circles.

Somewhere there had to be a comfortable place sized to fit widows and special children who never grew up.

Disney World!

Melissa did not like airplanes in any size, shape or color, so I decided that the Auto Train would do just fine.

I made reservations, packed the car and the two of us sped off on a sunny morning the day before Christmas. Melissa wore a big smile on her face. I wore a large sweater and a small frown as I watched our car loaded in Lorton, Virginia.

Melissa practiced sliding the doors open to our roomette. I practiced walking through each car with a babbling Melissa in tow to search out the dining car. Suddenly the train lurched forward. The ground sped away underneath the shuddering train. Melissa got so excited that it took me half an hour in the Observation Car to calm her down.

Dinner was uneventful. Despite my inner churnings, Melissa's unquenchable spirit continued to shine.

Melissa loved Christmas. Although she has little under-standable speech, she knew exactly what season this was. The music over the speakers and the festive mood shouted Christmas.

"Is Santa Claus coming to your house tomorrow?" our seatmates asked.

Melissa shook her head back and forth vehemently.

"But it's Christmas!" they protested. "It's Santa Claus's birthday!"

Melissa shook her head and pointed up to the sky.

"Melissa knows that Christmas is Jesus' birthday. I think that is what she's trying to say." I was afraid I sounded awfully pious.

The couple looked distressed and did not pursue any more conversation. Back in our roomette, Melissa and I stared at one another. There was no room for us to sit down or stand up. The two chairs were gone. They had been transformed into two narrow bunks with clean sheets.

"Melissa, where did we hide your suitcase?"

But Melissa had already climbed on the lower bunk and squirmed into her nightie.

"Melissa, the top bunk is yours!"

But Melissa was adamant. No way was she about to give up her exciting window to the world for a dark hanging shelf up near the ceiling.

"I'll be home for Christmas," the radio wailed. The familiar tune caught me off guard. What was I doing standing here, hanging on for dear life, trying to climb into a strange swaying target called bed?

Wrestling with my sweater, tugging at my stockings, I worried about climbing up those swinging canvas stairs. Taking a deep breath, I hoisted myself up and laid my round body flat, fearful of turning sideways lest I wedge myself forever against the ceiling.

At midnight, Melissa was still babbling at Christmas lights and railroad crossings. I climbed backwards down the swinging stairs to shuffle through the darkened corridor to the tiny bathroom at the end of the car.

When I returned, Melissa was still plastered against the cold window, watching the sights from the window.

"Move on over, Honey," I cheerily announced. "I can't climb up one more time to that top bunk."

Pushing and twisting, head to toe, we laughingly managed to fit. Soon Melissa's happy sounds became a part of my unending dreams.

Before we knew it, the Amtrak train jolted to a full stop.

It was Christmas morning! Melissa and I looked out of the window. There was nobody unwrapping presents, nobody baking pies in the kitchen, no friends in sight. Only strangers in a place called Sanford. A place where all the trains came to rest before they turned around and headed north again.

When at long last the busy attendants rolled our Buick down the ramp, Melissa gave a shout of glee and grabbed my hand.

"Bet you thought you'd never see our car again, did you, Melissa?"

By the time we found our motel, we were too tired to tackle the parks and settled for a swim and a nice dinner. The next morning, we went to Epcot. But even on some of the tamer rides, Melissa put her head down in my lap. The noises were deafening. So Melissa and I shuttled over to Fantasy Land where we were more at home.

We sang, "It's a Small, Small World," rode with Peter Pan, flew with Dumbo, and stayed on the carousel until Melissa's eyes shone again.

Back at the hotel, a swim in the golf course-sized pool revived our spirits. Later we snuggled in bed and watched a movie on TV. After three days more of swimming and sunning and meeting Mickey Mouse, we were ready to head home.

The first thing we spotted upon our return home was the Christmas tree. Melissa squatted down on the floor in front of it and looked with wonder at the perky red plaid bows and twinkling lights. I eased my weary bones into my favorite rocker, shook off my shoes and wiggled my toes gratefully.

Melissa played on the floor happily with her doll. I watched with amusement as her eyelids grew heavier. Finally she surrendered and laid her head contentedly on the pillow that I tossed down.

The big house was quiet. But it was a comfortable quiet. One that would soon fit my aching heart. I switched on the stereo to my favorite station and smiled as I heard the familiar, "I'll Be Home for Christmas." This time there were no tears. Can it possibly be? So far to go to know what that really meant! Home is where the heart is at rest. Paul was at home in Heaven, and Melissa and I were where his memories lived on. Home for Christmas at last!

> *But those who hope in the LORD will renew their strength.*
> *They will soar on wings like eagles;*
> *They will run and not grow weary,*
> *They will walk and not be faint (Isaiah 40:31).*

God has much to say about running, but my very favorite verse that provides more strength and comfort for my soul is this promise:

> *"The name of the LORD is a strong tower; the righteous run to it and are safe" (Proverbs 18:10).*

And inside my head and heart, I ran. I was safe. I called out, "Home free!"

I wondered what kind of Christmas Paul was having.

CHAPTER EIGHT

You're Going to Be a ... What?

*O*ne afternoon I had a visitor, an old friend who had worked side by side with us in the founding days of Melmark. In fact, Fran was our very first nurse. I shall never forget her. Unruffled, calm in the midst of unsettling circumstances, her manner was direct and honest. She told it like it was. The day she announced (after five years of Melmark duty) that she was leaving to be a missionary in Africa, I remember thinking that would be the end of Melmark. Clearly we could not exist without her. But she did—and we did!

Over bottomless cups of coffee that day, we talked of what I was going to do next. She felt that since God had left me here, He must have something for me to do.

She said, "Miggy, there are opportunities overseas for volunteers who just want to serve as a missionary for a short period of time. Why don't you visit the Africa Evangelical Fellowship at their offices in South Carolina?"

The idea zinged right to the core of me.

"They'd never take anyone as old as me, would they?"

And boom! She came right back at me with, "Well, you sure won't know unless you ask, now will you?"

This time, I called a family meeting. They all thought I had taken leave of my senses, but one month later, I climbed in the car and made the 700-mile trip to South Carolina.

I sat down with Wally, their friendly Candidate Director.

"How long has it been since my Paul—died?" I gulped. "I know you are thinking this is a knee-jerk decision."

"This is a big decision, you know, to go to Africa for even a short term of service. Are you certain that this is where God wants you to be?"

"There is only one thing I know for sure. God does not want me to curl up in some corner and wait to die. I can help out there in lots of ways … take care of children, tell them Bible stories, work in the kitchen. I have too much energy left to just sit in a rocking chair. Please don't tell me that is all there is for me now."

But Wally simply smiled and somehow I felt accepted already.

Before I left for home, I had enrolled in their two-week orientation scheduled for June. Yes, I was the oldest applicant. But nobody seemed to care. They called me their missionary with advanced mileage.

In June I went down again for a two-week orientation in South Carolina. Everybody everywhere was so breathlessly young. But we had a great time together, and I felt accepted in a new and exciting way. And then came the most important meeting of all—the meeting with the Board of Directors.

It was THE meeting everyone feared the most—the time when candidates told their stories and explained why they wanted to be missionaries. This was when the board determined who was suited for the mission field.

And now it was my turn. Twelve men sat around a big long table made into a square with me at the top of the square. They asked me to tell about my life.

I told them about the death of our baby Martha, the birth of our retarded child Melissa, and my Paul's death. They kept touching their hankies and swiping at their eyes. I tried not to look.

When I finished, nobody spoke. I couldn't stand it. This was the moment they were supposed to vote for or against me. But nobody made a move or even looked as if they were going to.

"Okay," I said it softly, "all in favor raise your hand!" I raised my hand up in the air.

Maybe they thought I was brash. But when I looked up, all I could see were their big smiles and their hands—in the air. I thanked them profusely. From that moment on, I was accepted. Wow!

Before the two weeks of orientation were over, an unusual opportunity presented itself. In the list of needs from Zambia, there was a small ad that appeared innocent but then blossomed into a full-blown opportunity. A primary school teacher with experience and initiative was needed for Mukinge Hill Academy, Mukinge, Zambia, to develop the program and play a vital part in making it possible for

Zambian professionals to stay in this rural area.

Well, believe me, it almost took my breath away. I didn't exactly have an official teaching degree, but I had done some substitute teaching eons ago in New Jersey. That should count for something. Besides, I love children. I was a grandmother to eleven grandchildren.

So I took the first step. I just knew, that at the very least, I had to try.

Well, the next steps came at me so fast they almost suffocated me.

Working with their travel director, I was scheduled to leave on a British Airways plane on the 4th of January bound for London, England. Could this really be happening? Without Paul? Without my right arm? How could I possibly manage alone?

Armed with eighteen immunizations, six U-haul boxes of household odds and ends and one over-sized duffel bag threatening to burst, I tearfully said good-bye to my family and my too-comfortable surroundings and traded them all in for a massive dose of the unknown.

I felt our kids all secretly thought I had gone off the deep end. That this was something I had to get out of my system—like a contagious disease.

Trying to look like a seasoned traveler, pulling my carry-on behind me, I wondered nervously where I had stashed the camera. Suddenly all the seat numbers blurred through my tears, and I could not seem to find my assigned seat. Everyone was surely laughing at this old lady stumbling down the aisle. My face got even redder as my *New York Times* slid to the floor, followed by the contents of my upside-down pocketbook. I did not dare look around.

After an all-night flight I had an all-day layover in London. I even managed to switch airports. There it was that I met another short-term missionary bound for the same mission station that I was. Jenny was young, blonde, beautiful and hailing from the state of Washington.

"Miggy!" She fairly bounced with excitement as we stood there hugging.

"Did you know that we are going to be next-door neighbors?"

I wasn't sure. For my first lesson in Zambian culture was that nothing was ever certain! But I could not have had a better (nor more beautiful) neighbor!

I hate to admit it, but I dreaded the twelve-hour trip to Lusaka. I prayed that I would not be hemmed in with passengers on every side. As I watched the passengers file in, stashing their belongings overhead, I knew it would be a full flight. Miracle of miracles the middle seat right next to me was vacant. Next to that there was an eight-year-old boy of seeming African heritage. I did not exchange anything with him but a tentative smile.

After a few hours in flight, I looked at him and said, "You know, we are lucky to have this empty seat right next to us. I know—we shall divide it up and you can have half and I will take half."

He liked that idea and plunked a few books down on his side as if to plant a stake with his property. We grinned at one another.

"Do you know how to play Crazy Eights?" he ventured.

So, after the movie had played the credit lines, the lights were dimmed, and the plane seemed subdued, we talked together very quietly as he taught me his game. People sprawled all over their seats with feet and heads hanging in the aisles. Jenny was already asleep in a kitty-corner seat.

The twelve hours passed quickly. God is mindful of His people.

"And surely I am with you always, to the very end of the age" (Matthew 28:20).

CHAPTER NINE

Out of Africa

anding in Lusaka, my eyes took in every sight. The first thing that hit me was the fact that nothing seemed to be working—not the elevators, the escalators nor the baggage carousel. Next, everywhere I looked I saw people, people, people. Everyone talking excitedly at once, filling up the aisles.

Jenny and I made our way toward the baggage claim area in a kind of dazed stupor. Waiting for our baggage to be brought down to the carousel that stood by silently, we met our missionary hosts, Keith and Judy. Big smiles and open arms made us forget we had never seen them before.

Their missionary assignment was to serve as host and hostess to missionaries coming and going to or from the field. Their personalities uniquely qualified them for their duties. The field headquarters for the mission was located in Chambra Valley, about fifteen minutes away. Still in the heart of the city, we noticed that most homes were

completely enclosed by high walls and locked gates. Inside
the fenced enclosures dogs paced back and forth, barking
whenever strangers approached. I deduced that security was
a big issue. I later discovered that food and soft goods were
attractive targets.

Then we arrived at the mission compound. Seven small
white cottages stood on slabs of cement as guest homes for
traveling-through missionaries. No screens but bars on the
open windows, all the necessary furniture, and bunk beds. I
drew in a quick breath and held it. Two sets of bunk beds! I
panicked.

Now, I have a social problem—I snore. This, my grandchildren attest to. There was not a safe haven here. I was
about to be revealed. This was going to be a three-day stopover
where we would shop for groceries and get over any jet lag.
That first night, however, pure exhaustion took over and I
forgot to worry. The next morning, I did not even ask if my
snoring had bothered anyone. It was nothing I could disguise
anyway.

Then, off for a shopping spree at the Shop-Rite. The
place was crowded. I could hardly push my cart in any one
direction. I kept saying "Sorry" to everyone I met. But most
seemed friendly, if a bit aimless.

I noted that all the young men seemed to be wearing
knit snow hats and white shirts. They were milling about,
tapping on the car windows in the parking lot, trying to
help you, begging for money. Judy suggested that we not
look at them so we were not forced to answer them. It was
one of the most difficult things I had to do. Here I had

flown across the ocean just to be one more person to turn them down, to say no to them. What a contradiction!

Three days later, we left on a single engine plane with bags of groceries and three other missionaries for Mukinge Mission Station. Mukinge was over 200 miles away in the bush. Because of my "advanced mileage" status, I was always assigned to the front seat. I did not mind one little bit.

When we were airborne, I could not stop looking at the beautiful landscape. Every clump of trees seemed to be a herd of elephants to me, and I am afraid I chattered most of the way. It was about a two-hour flight.

"Look down, that's Mukinge!" our pilot Phil said. Encircled by big, rounded hills in a valley, the school, the hospital and the houses of staff and teachers clumped together. We landed on a bumpy grassy strip of open ground behind the hospital.

And there stood Fran. Not soon will I forget her, surrounded by all the people who were waiting for someone ... anyone I guess. Not me, however.

We hugged and hugged. Fran was my key to everything there—where to shop, where to go to church, where to go to school, and where to find someone to play Scrabble® with. In my opinion, Fran topped the list of what a missionary should be.

I was in Africa! *What in the world was I doing here?*

I settled right next door to Jenny in a well-equipped apartment, designed for short-termers. And, sadly, there were no elephants nibbling my petunias or gangly giraffes peeking in my windows.

On Monday morning, barely two days after my arrival, timid knocks at my front door awakened me. There stood seven Zambian students with seven smiles. They hung their heads and said their names softly.

"You can call me Mrs. K." And they all giggled and took off their shoes.

"Oh, you don't have to take your shoes off," I said.

But they did. I was impressed.

"I just have to take my vitamins and brush my teeth. Then I'll be ready."

Gulping the last of my Zambian coffee, I remembered to take my anti-malaria drugs while trying to find out on Voice of America if Clinton had been impeached or if the stock market had crashed.

I learned a few of their names, stumbling over the pronunciation.

Pakasa and Chi-Chi each grabbed one of my hands. Kakenza insisted on carrying my basket filled with school supplies. Matonge toted my umbrella (it was the rainy season), and off we set for the little white schoolhouse half a mile up a slippery, muddy road.

Each day school began at 8:00 and ended at 1:00 in the afternoon. Eleven boys and girls, ranging in age from four through seven years of age, were my responsibility. Drew, a Canadian pre-med student, taught thirteen older ones.

I confess I fell in love with my students from the get-go. In their eyes, I was Mother Theresa, Princess Di, or a retired clown ... all rolled into one, and that was quite enough for me.

That I might show Christ to them daily was my desire. That I did it poorly is my confession. That I was happier than I have been in a long time was the banner waving over me.

I marched steadily onward. I read, played games, sat on the floor, made faces, told Bible stories, taught the alphabet and sang all sorts of silly songs with them. And I loved being a kid again with them. Did I feel like a missionary? Not one bit!

And exactly what does a missionary feel like? Oh, I guess I had rather a narrow definition of some long-faced lady with a serious frown, little laughter, and no time for the kind of fun I was enjoying.

My biggest stumbling block was, "What in the world do I eat that I really want to eat?" With the elevation at 4,300 feet, I had more than my allotted baking disasters. My confidence in my cooking ability plummeted. I invited folks to dinner with fear and trembling, and it was usually justified. Milk had to be pasteurized, drinking water boiled, and bread baked. My one fast food treat was a "meal-in-one" that they called "samosas," a delectable meat dish. This treat I could purchase from my Zambian neighbors. And, when all else failed, I had my jar of peanut butter. It was a battle of the bulge.

Was it hot? Considerably, but it usually cooled off at night. When the rainy season ended, we knew cooler weather was coming. I slept under a mosquito net and seemed to avoid the malaria threat. The lizards liked my apartment almost as much as I did. I zapped them with an electronic zapper.

But the flies were quite another subject! They were small in size, loud in noise and persistent. They preferred riding to flying, and what appeared to be a black shirt ahead of us on the road to school was simply one that was covered with free-riding flies. If I could not hear them buzz, I could assume they were plastered somewhere on my clothes. It was hard to shake them loose, but at least they were not buzzing in front of my face.

The snakes, however, seemed to be the biggest threat. Jabors, the man who slashed our grass, found and killed one four-foot king cobra trying to slither into my apartment under the back screen door. I immediately sealed off the gaps with cardboard and duct tape. We always carried torches (flashlights) at night so as not to step on them in the dark. Since I had no car, I walked wherever I went.

Drew, Jenny, and I became the incredible threesome, and never, ever did they make me feel like the odd man out. We usually ate our dinners together, and we pooled our supplies. That we could think of little else save chili and canned fruit and Jenny's ice cream did nothing to win us any culinary prizes. But we survived on our unimaginative diet and got numerous invites for dinner.

The Zambians proved to be hospitable and friendly, and we eagerly accepted their offers for meals. *Nshima*, which Drew liked better than Jenny or I did, was a corn-like mush that was the pre-determined dipper into the gravy or vegetables that accompanied the chicken. It was an art. Nshima was the centerpiece of each and every meal.

First, we passed the communal bowl of water around to

each one (guests were always first) to wash our hands. Then, and only then, did we gather round the table. Often the hosts would hover around and serve dinner. There was not quite enough room for everyone at the dinner table, but the warmth and love that surrounded us made even the awkward moments settle down.

The rolling of a ball of nshima was the tricky (and sticky) part. I never could get it right. Jenny was the pro. Drew just plastered a big smile on his face. Most often, I would sit with my left hand under me. That way only my right hand got sticky. I felt smug about this accomplishment, but nobody thought of it as a solution. After I waited a decent amount of time, I dipped my chunk into the gravy. By then nobody was paying attention. They just dove right in and rolled and dipped their way through dinner.

Warm homemade cake was a favorite ending to most meals, and we all went home feeling satisfied.

I tucked away all these unforgettable African experiences in my memory bank—memories that I did not share with Paul. I would have been doubly blessed to have had my tall husband by my side, smiling his way into the hearts of those Zambians. But wishing would never make it so.

CHAPTER TEN

The Sound of Silence

*A*lmost before I knew it, it was time for school holidays. One solid month off—away from the work that inspired me to cross the ocean. The schoolhouse closed its doors, the teachers were not needed. The kids went where all kids go when they have time off to share— to gather with their friends to play. I was thrown off balance, caught off guard.

So what does an unemployed teacher do? Read? Relax? Visit? But the other missionaries still were working at their respective assignments. So I was on my own.

When Jenny and Drew showed up for dinner that night just before our spring vacation, all they could chatter about was the trip planned by all the young people on the mission station—a real holiday—Victoria Falls and a safari at a wild game park. It sounded great and I cheered them on from the sidelines for Fran, my good friend, and I had planned a similar time away by ourselves a week or two later.

But life without Jenny and Drew was a shock.

When they left, the silent world oozed in. Would you believe it—the first stupid thing I did was to short-circuit my tape player? It hissed briefly before it died. Then the emptiness seeped in. It filled every cold corner of my little house and hid in every nook and cranny. I read voraciously from the stash of books that I had borrowed from other missionaries and even found myself reading the print on the cereal box.

Freed from the routine of the school day, I was like a wave tossed to and fro—nowhere to go, and no reason to go there. Fran still had her own missionary duties and the mile walk up the hill to see her could hardly be justified. Besides, I did not want anyone to see me on this slippery slide of despondency. The cement walls of the house were clammy, my feet were freezing and the relentless silence kept closing in on me.

My mind became a battlefield of doubts and fears. I cried into my pillow. I cried in the bathtub, and sometimes I did not even bother to wipe my tears.

What am I doing here? Am I really making a difference? I am surrounded by need on every side, but I am totally out of strength.

I knelt by my bed that night and told God about it. I showed Him my tears.

My pillow was damp.

He stretched out His arms.
"How can You still love me?" I cried out in wonder.
He showed me His hands.

"But, God, I can't go on. I am so tired."
He gave me His strength.

The hours crawled by. Each day I had energy enough for my tasks. One by one the days passed, and all too soon it would the 27th of May—my seventy-seventh birthday.

Then it was that I faced the future of my mission experience with naked honesty. I forced myself to realize what life would be like without Drew and Jenny, for their terms of service would soon be finished.

Finally, I sat down and wrote a dispirited letter to our field director, one of the kindest men in the world.

I told him I was homesick. I admitted openly that I wanted to go home. No, my term was not yet over, but only the one who wears the garment of life knows when his own fabric is weakening. I wanted nothing more than his blessing. That he answered my plea with graciousness and empathy crumbled me.

Soon it was the 27th of May. I celebrated my seventy-seventh birthday with my beautiful new friends—three parties and three cakes. A glorious mix of sadness with joy!

"Mrs. K. aren't you *ever* coming back?" Annie, one of Drew's students, said as big tears left wet paths down her dusty cheeks. I was ill-prepared for her overwhelming sadness.

Come June, I found myself seated again in the cockpit of the small mission plane leaving for Lusaka, heading for home.

My flight from London to Philadelphia on British Airways was doubly blessed. Seldom capable of sleeping on any plane,

I picked my way up the aisles at 2:00 A.M., dodging shoeless feet and bobbing heads. Outside the first class, a kindly attendant invited me to have a cup of tea with her. We stood there sharing bits and pieces of our lives. Then she asked me if I would like to try to sleep in first class. I was delighted.

"I'll make up a bed for you."

Soon my curiosity was satisfied. The "bed" stretched out at least six feet, and I gingerly lay down, not daring to peek around lest I be identified as a stowaway. It was so comfortable.

Two and one half hours later, I jumped up guiltily and left my delicious cove for my seat. My stolen sleep had satisfied that gnawing need for rest, and I thanked God for going above and beyond.

It was so good to feel the hugs of my family welcoming me home. But, true enough, among the glad welcomes, I again had to experience intrusive comments, this time prying into my reasons for leaving.

"I'm sorry things didn't work out for you in Africa."

These criticisms wedged themselves into my God-confidence, prying into what was a done deal between God and me. It nearly threw me off God-center.

Had I indeed bombed out? Had God accomplished what He wanted to? At my age, it sounds foolish to say that I found out who I am. For the last eight years, I had become so entangled with my role as a caregiver that I failed to anticipate my own needs. I had expected my grown-up, married children to fill in the blanks. Now I know that God intends me to lead my own life, depending on Him. Even to the point of not allowing the opinions of others to disrupt what He tells me in the quiet of our times together.

It is as though I experienced a new birth kind of thing. He was growing me up for widowhood. I had a new focus. Material things had somehow lost their insistence.

I may never be in Africa again, but whatever, wherever, I am learning to walk again on my own two feet—alone! Yet, not really alone, but with Him, every minute!

Was it all worth it? Had I made any difference at all?

Only God weighs the fruits of our labors and determines what is hay and what is stubble. It was mine to offer and His to bless. He trusted me with this unexpected adventure at a rather advanced age.

Would I ever go back to Africa? In a heartbeat—were it not for my thirty-eight-year-old daughter with Down's syndrome. Melissa doesn't miss a step when I'm gone, but I am the one who longs for her.

As for me, God is proving Himself to me. He shows me each and every day that as long as I am still breathing, He has given me a life that is meant to be lived to the fullest. He will open doors for me at any age. His love is enough. His kindness wraps me up, and His strength makes me walk and not faint.

"But those who hope in the LORD will renew their strength. They will soar on wings like eagles; they will run and not grow weary, they will walk and not be faint" (Isaiah 40:31).

CHAPTER ELEVEN

"God, Where Are You?"

*T*he first Sunday back in Pennsylvania, Melissa and I went to church. We stood in the beautiful sanctuary that had been finished in my absence and Melissa said one word: "WOW!" Indeed, it was majestic! Our new abode all finished with pews, choir loft, stained glass window, and a magnificent organ.

But why did it suddenly make me want to get up and run away? Back to that little church in Mukinge, back to the simplicity of housedresses and bare feet? Back to not looking all around wondering who was or wasn't there? My soul was yearning for the continuation of that unfinished journey— that quiet timelessness that was Africa.

The local church in Mukinge was located up that same dirt road I walked every day to school. Except it was further up the hill. Trudging through the long grass in the shortcut, the aroma that wafted across the open fields each and every Sunday announced that you were almost there.

Inside you forgot about it when the singing started. Never before had I heard such heart-warming singing. Tears ran unchecked down my hot cheeks. We squeezed together on wooden benches with no backs. The room was filled with people, men and women, young and old, but decidedly more of the latter.

In addition to the distraction of the heat, there were of course, the flies. The unscreened windows were open in hopes of catching a stray breeze. Colorful headdresses matched cotton housedresses, and bare feet made me envious that I had not thought to do the same. Everyone seemed happy and comfortable. No matter that I did not know the lyrics of the hymns, many of the tunes were familiar to me. So I sang in English, and they sang in Kikaonde. But, did it matter?

Two short pews in the back sported nice rounded backs. We had to get there first in order to get those, but no one showed any reticence in crowding just one more person on the pew. They were the best seats in town, as well as being the only seats where Fran's feet could reach the floor.

Why didn't I feel just as comfy or at ease in my own home church? I missed the love, the fellowship, and the openness of Africa.

"God, where are You?"

I don't know whatever prompted me to stumble down the valley of doubt. I felt a million miles away from God. I looked for blessing and level pathways in front of me, but unexpected trials appeared around every corner.

God seemed to hide Himself in the shadows. I could not see Him, I could not find Him and sometimes I didn't even want to. I read the story of the crucifixion and nothing stirred within me. I feared my tomorrows.

Have I lived too long?

For what will He send my way now? One night I picked up the "Hound of Heaven" by Francis Thompson and read it through. Again! It is quaint writing with impassioned rhetoric filling every little page. But even as I read, my heartbeat thundered in my ears. I read it again and tears filled the well of my eyes. I sat there in the silence, and I thought I heard God speaking to me. I felt His nearness. His love surrounded me and caught me by surprise. Now the tears knew no stopping point. They fled down my cheek.

Listen to these words in the middle of the poem:

All which I took from thee I did but take
Not for thy harm, but that thou might'st seek it in My arms—
All which thy child's mistake fancies as lost,
I have stored for thee at home ...

God was simply storing my treasure in Heaven where neither moth nor rust can corrupt.

How strange that I should be seeking my Heaven—on earth! How unceasingly stupid I was. What is Heaven for? God was guarding my treasures for me. My tiny six-month old baby snatched from my arms before her life had begun ... my daughter Melissa, so handicapped in her mind ... my husband struck down so that there was nothing left but his frail body.

God, You knew how I had looked forward to those golden years with my husband. But now this big old house is filled with nobody but You and me. Even You, dear God, are sometimes far away. I cannot find You because I have filled my heart with noisy things that crowd You out of my life. The radio, the television, the phone calls and the books I read which know You not. They are all intruding on my God-space.

Oh God, my Hound of Heaven, I bow before You. My heart and soul crumble.

Make of me what You want to. Take what You want of my life, my fancied treasures. The radio, the television, the phone calls, and the books I read that do not know You. You are all I want, all I want.

God, thank You for catching me. Thank You for reminding me that I am just passing through. There is so much to worry about. What will I do if my money runs out? Who will take care of me? I would like to invite myself into Your Home, God, but I think I must have things that You want me to do yet.

Just stay close by me, God. I can only get through it if You help me.

Clearly God intends me to live my life right up to the end of it. Not squirming into some dark corner but to continue to be of use to Him.

CHAPTER TWELVE

Who Cares?

*D*ay after day passed. As the months disappeared, I noted with great alarm my accumulation of extra weight. It hadn't happened overnight, but it surely caused me to look in the mirror twice. What would Paul say if he were alive?

I had been through all the diets I knew about and skipped down all those miracle trails that eager advisers told me about—all to no avail.

It had started with a short visit in the hospital for a runaway pulse and high blood pressure. The cardiologist told it like it was. I happened to read his notes (upside down, of course). In answer to one question, he had written a short five-letter word: *obese!* I tried to laugh, but this was not really humorous. So I swallowed my pride in silence.

Sitting there in my well-worn slippers and oversized bathrobe, I remembered I had no makeup on to cover those horrible brown spots on my face. And then I discovered an amazing secret—sitting down made me feel younger cause I couldn't tell where my stomach ended and my legs began. And when my body leaned forward expectantly and my hands gestured expressively, amazing! I *acted* young!

But then it was a horse of a different color when I stood up. Pulling, no, yanking on the back of whatever I was wearing to make certain that it was not bunched, I didn't bother sucking in my tummy anymore. I couldn't do it for very long anyway.

Going on a crash diet one week only caused me to gain four pounds. It was amazing.

"I must have a tape worm," I confided to the doctor.

"No." He gave it some serious thought and, bless him, he didn't smile. "But perhaps your metabolism is a bit off. We shall test your thyroid."

Marvelous diplomat! That was it, of course. I could think that way for a solid week until my test results came it. Then a reality check sent me sleuthing for clothes that would fit.

Shopping that day was a rude awakening. The air became oppressive in the tiny changing room. And my cheeks reddened when the salesgirl brought in some dresses marked Size 1X. Could it be?

"Oh, these are the wrong size!" I protested softly, scared that maybe they really weren't.

"Well, let's just try them, shall we? They are really just the next size after 16," she offered.

They fit! I never said a word.

Determined to make those pounds disappear and confident of the fact that I was not honoring God with this extra poundage, I set out with gusto to swim at the YMCA. They offered swimming for older active adults from 12:00 to 1:00 P.M. on Monday, Wednesday, and Friday. This I could do.

I was assigned my clothes locker and handed a combination lock, the likes of which I had not seen since high school. The locker room at the Y was comfortably filled with women of all sizes, all of whom seemed to have known each other for ages. They talked a mile a second and walked around without a towel—stark naked.

"Well, I guess I was born thirty years too soon," I murmured under my breath.

Nobody was embarrassed, except me, and nobody thought she had anything to hide, except me. I found a neglected corner and, eyes down, I managed to get the bottom layer of my clothes off.

Quickly pulling my bathing suit on, I shed my sweatshirt and headed for the pile of towels. They did little to hide my agony, but I draped one casually over a shoulder and boldly headed for the pool. Only about ten, or at the most fifteen, people were there, so we had the entire pool to wallow around in and a lifeguard to boot. What we needed one for is beyond me, since few ventured beyond the shallow end. Many had all their makeup on and their hair had obviously just been combed.

I didn't know a soul so I ducked under the water and swam to the deep end where I could lose myself in a million thoughts.

What made God think of water? Floating blissfully on my back, I thought of all the times He went to the lake or on a boat

*to retreat from the crowds that were following Him. And how
scared the disciples were when they saw Jesus walking on the
water. They were three and a half miles out to sea, mind you,
when that happened.*

Down at the shallow end there was a loosely gathered
circle of swimmers with a white-haired gentleman leading
some rather strenuous exercises. At this point, I thought I had
better join them. They surely must be thinking I was a snob,
too good to join their circle. I swam closer and tried to catch
somebody's eye. But everybody was watching some other
body and that body was not me. Finally, I just spoke out
and let the question float in the air.

"May I join your circle?"

They welcomed me, grunting or nodding their heads,
and they never skipped a beat. They then started doing some
sort of ostrich or pelican thing under the water. I could not
see what they were doing, but they sure acted very intent
and preoccupied. So I swished around a bit and splashed
noisily all the while frowning hard as though concentrating
on what I was doing. What, I had not the slightest idea.

After a while, I caught on. Just when I was feeling comfortable and part of the group, some lady started singing
out loud: "Did you ever see a lassie?" and then, "Zip-ah-
de-doo-dah," swinging into a rousing finale of "You are my
sunshine."

It struck me as funny and sad in a nostalgic way. She was
being who she was and singing the songs she knew without
an outside thought as to who was there listening. Even the
bemused look of the young lifeguard was not a deterrent.

He simply looked as though he might join in at the chorus. I finally added my alto to the other voices who had already joined in.

I was grateful that nobody was there to evaluate the worth of my swimming regime to my weight-loss program. But I had a great time.

I got to thinking about God and His plan for each one of us. Who holds us accountable? How strictly do we follow what we know He wants for our lives? It is not an easy thing to live the Christian life. Don't ever let anyone deceive you. It requires discipline and adherence to His rules for our lives.

What we must remember is that His plan always works. It is individualized, customized and guaranteed to fit. Not like those garments that boastfully assert they will fit one and all. They hang on the rack, looking as if surely they could do the trick, but you and I know differently.

I came across this verse:

"Their destiny is destruction, their god is their stomach, and their glory is in their shame" (Philippians 3:19).

I hung my head, but if I needed reassurance that God had not given up on me, it was also there in His Word.

"Man looks at the outward appearance but the LORD looks at the heart" (1 Samuel 16:7).

Clearly the ball was in my court.

It dawned on me that this was just one more issue that had heretofore been much easier when Paul was alive. He had made the difference. Not a morning passed without his verbal assurance that he loved me. He would also comment on what I was wearing. I had grown to count on this and, in its absence, missed the accountability it demanded of me. The results had been disastrous. I know now that we need one another to encourage each other.

"Do you not know that your body is a temple of the Holy Spirit, who is in you, whom you have received from God?" (1 Corinthians 6:19)

Would I forever miss Paul and the special magic he put in our lives together?

CHAPTER THIRTEEN

Moving On

*S*uddenly I was getting ready to celebrate my eighti-
eth birthday. As I looked around me, it seemed that
many of my friends had either gone on ahead or were settling
back for the good life. It was a bit depressing. The widows I
knew were shutting their front doors, moving in with their
children and hanging the sign, "Closed for Business" in their
window. And it caused me to wonder. Is this the life that
God wants for them? For me?

Perhaps because I felt that there was still something left
for me to do and new horizons to scope out, I wanted to
keep on full speed ahead. I needed to at least discover what
God had in mind for the rest of my life. After all, why would
God leave me behind if there were nothing He had in mind
for me to do?

*"I am the LORD your God, who teaches you what is best
for you, who directs you in the way you should go" (Isaiah
48:7).*

Eighty! A startling number. As I rounded out my seventies, the eighties promised to be a decade of change. The biggest change and accompanying adjustment was my decision to move from the campus of Melmark where I had lived for thirty-five years. Leaving my friends at Melmark who had stood shoulder to shoulder helping us get started was not easy. They did not all understand why I was leaving.

I made the decision, with the help of family, to move to a retirement community in Rexford, New York, a rural upstate community very near to my daughter Diane. I felt the situation was sized to fit.

But there was no way to ready myself for the change. First came the inevitable thinning down of all that I possessed. The chafing dish, the punch bowl, those party things for which there was no room. I passed them on. And there was pleasure in that, for all the married grandkids starting out to keep house needed so much. So I was glad to help.

But it was confusing. I hardly knew what I was doing. So when the packers asked me whether or not I wanted to keep some article, I just said no. It was easier and besides, it really did not matter. They were just things, nothing more. And things can get cumbersome. Someone must dust them or find a place to hide them. Better to forget about them— they were not worth my time. Diane and my daughter-in-law Ruth stepped in to help. (Understatement there!) Never could I thank them enough.

But what about leaving Melissa? For the last thirty-eight years, Melissa had been the focal point of our lives. After

Paul died, she assumed the throne quite smoothly. Oh, our conversations were meaningless, our laughter foolish, but our friendship was real. I could always count on her. But now I was the faithless one. I was leaving her. Would she miss me or was the lonesomeness all on my side? If I could just have one more hug, would that satisfy me? Seemed I had carved out another empty hole in my life.

But in the cold light of a new morning came the reality that I could not ever supply for her the wholesomeness that is Melmark. That is an intrinsic part of her happiness. Her peers who accept her frailties without question, laugh at her sense of humor, and indulge her eccentricities—those I cannot ever provide. She is freer to be herself in the loving environment that is Melmark than all the community-like things I can provide.

For often when Melissa and I are out in the world, shopping or dining out together, just about anywhere in the public eye, I see people watching her. They seem to snap to attention whenever they pick up on one smidgin of her abnormal behavior. They watch and stare. While Melissa does not even notice, it sends my alarm system to shrieking.

Oh, ye watchers of others, ye scrutinizers of all behaviors— what is it you demand? Sameness? Walk on by, for now you can find only the widow—sad in countenance, bereft in heart and empty of spontaneity. Long ago fashioned to walk without stumbling, talk without stuttering and eat with closed lips and puckered brow. Stripped of trying to protect the weaker one, yet now even becoming the weaker one day after day. Alone in the middle of a crowd of others much like herself—different sizes and assorted shapes, fitting in whenever necessary and escaping only to the mountain of many words where ideas float like zombies.

So, I moved to Coburg Retirement Village, outwardly conforming, inwardly still questioning. It is a community equipped for the active older adult, with no assisted or nursing home care offered. The part I like best is that one meal a day is offered in a most pleasant dining room, with three enjoyable choices for the entrée.

At Coburg I am a nonentity. No past history, no portfolio, and no future—for what goals can an eighty-year-old possibly achieve? When you live in a world where no one understands your past or even cares about it, it is comforting to know that God cares. People ask why I moved so far away from Melmark, and it is just too complicated and not important any more.

I have relocated.

CHAPTER FOURTEEN

Life on the Compound

*M*y very first evening at Coburg I climbed the sweeping front stairs to the dining room. I stood in the wide doorway waiting to be seated. The room was filled with at least a hundred widows with a few widowers thrown in. Women of assorted ages and sizes with gray or white hair, curled tightly or swept up in a gorgeous chignon or some with hair combed simply forward, hugging their heads like a helmet.

I was riveted to the spot, realizing that I was just another ancient pilgrim in that sea of senior citizens. Listening to the pleasant buzz of conversation, I really did not know what to do next.

No announcements! No trumpet flourish—just a widow, scared to pieces. Where should I look? With whom was I to eat? Who would tell me what was needed here?

Here I was, separated from my home of the last thirty-five years, away from the one child left in our family who really needed me. Here in a rural area of upstate New York feeling completely out of place. Here with 170 other people in the same boat. Some with eyes blinded by a blurring of vision, loins slipping into blubbery plumpness (well, mine anyway), and minds teetering on the edge. Who said that I wanted to spend the rest of my life living with everyone the same age that I was?

Well, evidently I had. My memory had not yet slipped its moorings. I did remember that. This was just entry panic.

Walking toward me came a lady who looked interesting and seemed to be operating at full horsepower. Someone I would like to know better.

"Hi!" I ventured. "Are you waiting for someone better to come along?"

She laughed—a very ladylike laugh, and walked on by.

The head waiter seated me on the veranda at a table for two but at the moment accommodating only an unhappy me. I wondered, *how do I get dining partners?* Do I line them up ahead of time? But I did not even know anyone's name. *Small problem there.* I said hello to everyone I saw and smiled my most engaging smile, but no takers. Oh well, another hurdle.

Over the weeks ahead I observed a certain sameness. It frightened me. Everyone doing everything in the same old way. They all were fitting in. They seemed to eat with the same people most every night. I was sure there was some-one out there who needed a friend. Was it kosher to pray that I might find that person? How could I break into their established routine?

I looked around at dinner time and saw those who sat and

stared at their dinner plates throughout dinner, lost in the wonder of dementia, hardly remembering to pick up their fork. Others were constantly on the lookout, scanning the tables for something new, something startling. Perhaps some grist for the rumor mill? *Unfair observation there!* And finally the widowers who ate together at one table, fighting to keep their independence, afraid their mere presence will create a feeding frenzy among all the gussied-up widows.

There were also those who broke my heart—the crippled in mind or body. Their conversation was often limited or non-existent, but the moment their meal was over, they stood up shakily and instinctively their hands reached out to find each other. These were the brave ones. The husband whose head shook constantly, the wife who was bent over with osteoporosis. But, they had each other. I wondered if they appreciated that. Sure one of them might be hurting in body or mind, but hey, they could snuggle together in their little apartment. They could keep each other warm.

There were those folks whose eyes were bright and knowing, whose manners were impeccable, whose appearance was noteworthy. They led a full life at Coburg. They played bridge, did crosswords, shopped in interesting places and lunched in out of the way restaurants. Almost as though their husbands were here. To them I gave full credit.

That they were able to sift the wheat from the tares made their contribution to the world of the handicapped that much more laudable. They stepped up to bat and filled in the gaps in other peoples' lives when the doing was less than glorious. I admired them from afar. I did not greet them by name for

I did not know them that well. Perhaps someday.

And oh yes, the active couples who swam in the morning, held hands when walking together and smiled and chattered away contentedly. I envied them, sometimes I even begrudged them their lot in life. They did not look for dining partners—they had each other. Their home was filled with the joys and demands of life together as a married couple. Their step was full stride. If wishing made it so, I expected a lot of us would trade places with them for just a little bit. They seemed so complete. Seeing them, I yearned for Paul.

There were those who whined and complained about most everything and anything. It blows my mind when I think of trying to please all of us women with meals or anything else for that matter. How can any facility be all that everyone agrees upon? However, I am hard put to find much to complain about. The meals are well rounded and appealing, and there is always a choice. But why then is it somehow never the right one for some? Why is the soup always too cold, the ice cream too hard, the bread stale, and the meat tough. How dare they serve rice instead of potatoes?

It was hard to know how to respond to them. I wanted to ask those who complained two simple questions: "Who in the world gets what they want every time? Do you really believe you were promised a rose garden?"

But one thing we all seemed to share— the option to be the squeaky wheel or to be a part of the well-oiled machinery. Each person made a deliberate choice as to which side of the ledger to weigh in on. On the credit side were those who adjusted. It seemed a bit harder to find those who were completely content, not trying to run the place.

From my office window I often watched the residents at Coburg walking around the compound, heads braced against an unseen wind, teetering from side to side, slowly, oh so slowly. The fast ones strode by as though they were competing in a walking race. But, I noted that they were careful to greet each person. Sometimes they mouth a breathless "Hi" and other times they exchange observations about the weather.

Each morning I found it easy to retreat to my office and my writing. While my writing gave me purpose, I earnestly prayed that I was not just "counting peas." Walter Wangerin, one of my favorite authors said it so well in his book *Measuring the Days* (New York: HarperCollins Publishers, 1993, pp.276-277).

> In Albert Camus's novel, *The Plague*, an old man sits in his bed and counts peas from one pan to another, cheerfully as though the practice accomplished something. This is the way he divides his life: "Every 15 pans, it's feeding-time." This is the way he occupies himself until he shall die: "What could be simpler?"
>
> The narrator is impressed by the old man's honesty and self-awareness. Life holds no meaning whatsoever for this old man; therefore, he has created a ritual activity of nothingness: its meaning is to while away a meaningless time.

I pray that the words I pen have meaning and purpose—

that they bring enlightenment and encouragement to the reader. I pray that my writing has not just become a means of escaping interaction with real people or a way to fill hours until something meaningful comes along.

I pray that I am not just counting peas.

CHAPTER FIFTEEN

The Stone at the Bottom

I have twin heartaches. I keep them in locked boxes buried deep down inside of me. God knows all about them. We have cried and agonized over each one. He could remove them, but He does not. He may never. I know that. But it is hard, sometimes, to keep following Him with my heart so weighed down. Many times I feel like just collapsing in a small heap and weeping over them. But this is not good.

While I don't beg Him to take them away, I sure wish He would. I have told Him about the many ways I thought we could bring about some changes so that I could carry these heartaches more easily, but He tells me over and over to give them to Him. I do this repeatedly. I just don't seem to have enough sense to leave them alone. But He does not want me to try to fix them either. So I don't! I guess it's kind of what trust is all about. Follow the leader.

"I have set the LORD always before me. Because He is at my right hand, I will not be shaken. Therefore my heart is glad" (Psalm 16:8-9).

I will go forward under that banner and hold my head high. It is a promise, my prayer, and my plea. The situation has not changed. All things remain the same, and it seems they shall run their full course. I must not interfere. I simply wait before Him. Joy cometh in the morning. I will sit on the ash heap with Job and wait—and hope—and pray.

"Through all this Job did not sin nor did he blame God" (Job 1:22, NASB).

God knows best how to deal with each one of His people. For God seldom answers my specific prayers, and I am glad He does not. I am so conflicted, I want only chocolate with macadamia nuts swirled with marshmallows and peanut butter instead of plain ordinary chocolate—I want, I want, I want—I am sure I would turn into a manipulative renegade if allowed my own way.

He made me, and He knows me. He knows I am not one of His strongest Christians so He has permitted me to see the amazing outcome of some of the trials that befell me so that I could learn to trust Him when my vision was blurred. I never felt His absence, but only the presence of an all-knowing, all-wise God.

The birth of our handicapped daughter Melissa led to the foundation of Melmark, a home and school for 180 children and young people—a home for those with mental retardation, including those with medical, physical, and emotional problems.

Was all this using some talents that Paul and I already had? No, for we were not experienced except in the valley of tears—the tears we shed over the death of our baby Martha and the birth of our baby Melissa. But God interrupted my life and said, "Wait! I will show you something." And He did! God was our wisdom, our leader and CEO. And Melmark, home and school for the handicapped, is still operating at full speed thirty-seven years later. Not under our leadership now, but under God's umbrella.

Browning said it so well. He said that there were two kinds of sorrow, the escapable one and the inescapable. The escapable one is much like a death—as final as a slammed door. Like the unexpected death of our six-month old baby Martha who choked on a tiny bit of food in her trachea and died in her carriage on a sunny day in May. Just like that. And just like that my snug little world imploded. *What in the world was God doing?*

That was forty years ago and the piercing hurt of that moment has softened with the passing of time, and I can envision her baby plumpness now without completely disintegrating.

But an inescapable sorrow is much like an incurable illness, a physical deformity, or a mental disease. Or the Alzheimer's disease that consumed Paul or the Down's syndrome that even now hinders Melissa's progress beyond the world of a three-year-old.

As an illustration, Browning likens it to a stone thrown into a pool of water. The pool looks calm and serene on the outside, but as the stone enters, the waters part. The stone sinks to the bottom of the pool. Then, on the surface, all appears placid again. The waters have come together. But the stone remains at the bottom.

Here is where God steps in. He wants to be my stone-bearer.

"Come to me, all you who are weary and burdened, and I will give you rest" (Matthew 11:28).

God seldom removes the stone, but He is ready to carry it for me.

God bears the stone of my twin heartaches.

CHAPTER SIXTEEN

Time Out!

Good morning, God!

I do not know why I want to write this instead of just talking to You, but maybe in the midst of all the muddling around that my mind does, I want to make something very clear. I am painfully aware of the lack of fellowship that we have had lately. You always said that fellowship was a two-way street, but it almost looks as though I have set up roadblocks in front of my entrance. Proudly erected then, I faintheartedly try to tear them down now. They are not toppling easily.

I don't feel that tug in my innards toward You. I love You, but I have forgotten the freshness, the ardor of our love. I experience the warmth of Your support down in the valleys of my life, but honestly, I don't want to live down in the valley the rest of my life. Please no, God. I do not think that I would have the courage to endure. I would go down with a colossal bang and never get up again. Then You would be super disappointed in me.

I used to remember Your love letters by heart, but now my memory grows unreliable. They are all here. I could read them again. I have the time, but I keep putting them off. Later! But now, I must eat. I must have my breakfast.

Do You love me when I am like this? I wonder.

One day from my office window I watched the children of my neighbors closing off the last of their parents' lives. Their mother had died. She fell and went to the hospital, and now she is no more. It was very quick. That is the way these things happen around here. There was the ominous arrival of the ambulance, the wonder as to who it was, and then the departure of all the emergency equipment, leaving in its wake an unanswered question.

Then I saw the sons and daughters carrying out boxes from their mother's little cottage. The boxes were the good stuff. This they kept. Then I observed the enormous black bags of junk. These were her treasures. She thought they were important and went to all the trouble to catalogue them, but at the last, they never made the cut. Pure unadulterated junk, assessed with a quick eye for picking the good and pitching out the junk.

Back and forth they went into the cottage to search for treasure. They must have wondered why their mother's cottage was so messy. Now at last the truth had surfaced.

Soon the cottage looked better, but there was no life left. The blinds were squeezed shut. The lamps were switched off and behind them, the door closed with a final thud. I'm sure the house had already started to get very cold.

And that was the end of life for her. I wondered where she was. I had never even said hello.

That was the way my Monday started, and then the familiar sameness started to drip into my soul. *What of today? Will it be different? Where is Melissa? Why, when my arms long for her, is she not here? Does God long for me like that? Does He want me to be closer? Does He mind listening to me ramble? Wondering why I don't take up my bed and walk? How many half-alive dreams have I swept out of my heart? I'm sure He does not need me to carry out any of His plans, but oh, how I need Him.*

I don't know what pattern You are working on for me, but oh God, help me to be more pliable.

CHAPTER SEVENTEEN

Learning to Flex

I think I have been promoted from my kindergarten class in grief. At first, I was so upset when Paul died that I just wanted to wallow in my tears and live there. My own private swimming pool. But I knew that it was not a healthy thing to do. I felt I must move on. It was time for the mourning to cease occupying front and center stage.

I knew one friend who went on and on for months, years, before she pulled the shade down on her own grief. I did not understand why she wanted to remember the day, the hour, the very moment when something dreadful happened. Perhaps in "marking the moment" she forgot to move on.

> *Whatever is true, whatever is noble,*
> *whatever is right, whatever is pure,*
> *whatever is lovely, whatever is admirable—*
> *if anything is excellent or praiseworthy—*
> *think about such things*
> *(Philippians 4:8).*

God says it so succinctly. I wonder how I could have missed it. And for good measure, He says it again.

There is a time for everything, and a season for every activity under heaven: A time to be born and a time to die, a time to plant and a time to uproot, a time to kill and a time to heal, a time to tear down and a time to build, a time to weep and a time to laugh, a time to mourn and a time to dance (Ecclesiastes 3:1-4).

Along with all the missing pieces of my life's jigsaw, I find myself looking for those extra polite kindnesses that Paul did so naturally. I do not think he was aware that he was doing anything out of the ordinary.

Take parking for instance. Guess what? I despise parking my own car. As I plop one foot after another trudging down to that dreary lot, I admit to being envious of those complacent wives standing inside somewhere waiting for their husbands.

And I wonder if I will never ever get used to eating alone— in a restaurant. It's bad enough when you're alone at home, but when you're in some restaurant, it's just plain awful. I become fully convinced that everyone in the room is looking at and through me. And I don't know where to tell my eyes to go. I can't look directly at people, for that is incredibly rude, and I get tired of staring at the table. As for the menu, that only works until the waiter takes your order and whips it out of your hand. As a tiny means of coping, I try to bring along something to read, a paperback or at the very least last week's church bulletin—anything!

After more than five years of widowhood, I do still long for someone to park my car and dine with me, but I have also picked up some amazing new skills along the way. My portfolio is expanding. Maybe not in the ways some might call desirable, but I am kind of proud of some of my newly acquired skills.

Unassembled! That word alone used to send shivers down my spine. *Partially assembled*—was a little bit better, but almost just as challenging. Now I find I *can* read directions and use a screwdriver. I *can* figure out where A needs to be attached to B. Why did I always think that was Paul's job? I hid under the excuse of "Oh honey, you know I can't do that!"

Recently, I put together an unassembled desk, with a pullout shelf for my computer. Now, how cool is that!

I have also found out there is something else to be gained by being just one. I have time! A scarce commodity, it seems. Since I do not have to eat at any specified time, I am freer to offer rides to those who need it.

I try not to memorialize my sad days. I hear other widows talking—"It was exactly two months ago today that my husband died." Or, "This was the day the we went to the cemetery together—always on Memorial Day." I have been busy fashioning some new memories, and now I shall try to remember my happy days.

I do try to continue one of the things Paul and I did together during our "quiet times" together in the morning—

putting on the whole armor of God. Many times we forgot. Our feet got to going before our minds clicked in. Perhaps we thought there was not enough time on some busy mornings. Those were the times we delayed until the day was past and when the night came, we were so weary that we put God in His box until another more convenient time.

I am not proud of those times. But now, by myself, I try not to go out without my armor. If God has gone to the trouble of providing it, why would I leave it tucked in a corner of my Bible somewhere? I need protection.

Therefore, put on the full armor of God,
so that when the day of evil comes,
you may be able to stand your ground,
and after you have done everything, to stand.
Stand firm then, with the belt of truth buckled around your
      waist,
with the breastplate of righteousness in place,
and with your feet fitted with the readiness that comes
from the gospel of peace.
In addition to all this, take up the shield of faith,
with which you can extinguish all the flaming arrows of the
      evil one.
Take the helmet of salvation and the sword of the Spirit,
which is the word of God.
And pray in the Spirit on all occasions
with all kinds of prayers and requests.
With this in mind, be alert
and always keep on praying for all the saints
(Ephesians 6:13-18).

Whenever I forget my armor, forgetting about God for the moment, I find out that the next day, it is even easier to forget Him.

As I continue to adjust to my new world, I am also daring to drive long hours in the car alone. First, I lock my doors and avoid any highway confrontation. I have (mostly always) tried to maintain a speed somewhere near the speed limit. And I keep saying I will know when to stop driving when a lot of people beep at me. They have not done that yet. So I travel here and there unfettered.

I also try to avoid those friends who complain about everything that happens. They turn my grapes to sour, my wine to vinegar, and my smiles to frowns. Frequently this means I have had to go it alone. But God has a plan for me, and I know He will send the proper friend at the proper time.

Very often now I go out on a limb, attempting something brand-new, something I am not sure that I can do. I remind myself:

"If the only birds that sang were those that sang the best, the forest would be silent indeed."
"Don't miss the plum for want of courage to shake the tree."

Above all else, I remind myself of the fact that God is with me and is still in the business of caring for me whether I'm a single or a double. I am always amazed at the little surprises He has for me along the way.

And as I have had ample opportunity to flex my faith

muscles, I have found that I am stronger than I realize! Whenever I feel my knees quaking and my soul sinking through the floor, I gather myself and resort to God's Word.

CHAPTER EIGHTEEN

A New Assignment

*B*eing a widow is not easy ... sometimes it is down-right tough! The whole world seems just like a Noah's Ark to me, couples only. Sometimes I rebel at the world I live in. Not always, but frequently.

But here I am—bound by my own frailties. A widow, not by choice, but by design. God's! I am still breathing in and out, my heart is thumping away, and I am alive. God has given me day after day to live to the fullest. Why? Why hasn't He taken me home? Often I wonder.

I know that God has a reason!

But I sure don't know what it is. I tried one day to sit down and really think things through. Does God know what He's doing? In theory, I know the answer to that. So, then, I must find out what that is. Right? Sounds great on paper.

Physically, I'm falling apart. It isn't fun. I get the flu, catch everyone's cold, hesitate before I move, step—then stumble, and then totally forget where I am going. I feel like the biggest burden around.

I sit and waste the hours watching TV, play office at the desk shuffling all the mail four or five times, or curl up with a fast-moving book until it's time to go to bed again. Can God use a bent over, weak old widow for anything but a casket filler?

Yes!

To begin with—He made me. He knows my end from my beginning. He is the only One who can send out invitations to my going home party. That's because only He can fill in the exact time. Absolutely no point in my whining about the timing. God will not be hustled.

So, then, what shall I do about that? I don't want to fizzle out. Obviously!

He did not send me to earth just to fill up a space, to round out the census. God knows what He is doing.

But I think I've lost my dignity. This senior citizen, golden age propaganda is for the birds. I can't get into or out of the car without looking like a confused camel. The other end of the seat belt always seems out of reach while I fumble and flutter. I smile a lot because I really don't like my face when I don't. And my legs, whatever has happened to them? Where has all my get up and go gone? Why does God let old age be such a bummer? There must be an easier way to end our lives with some semblance of dignity.

And then I stop and remember what God did for me. God left His dignity and His kingdom by becoming a wee small baby. He was helpless, dependent, resorting to whimpers and cries for all His needs. That was His unexpected gift for His world—His life for mine. And now I am complaining for living so long? I have to remember Who He is. He's worth living for.

As I ponder, I mentally list all the pluses in my life, the gifts He has so generously given me. I love people, and many of His people are lonely and needy. I think perhaps if I brushed off my gift of hospitality, I could help someone. I have the time. I could make a cup of tea for that lonesome somebody who needs an excuse to pop in for longer than a moment.

"Do come over for a spot of tea." It can't be that hard for me—I could even make a banana muffin.

So many widows have super talents that they can use for God. I wish I could sing as they do. But sadly I can't do the solo thing, so I try to keep the pews warm.

I remember reading about that widow who made a special room for her friend, the prophet Elisha. She had a room set apart to make him feel welcome, just set apart for a weary stranger. That was a neat thing to do.

It seems that I have lived many years splattered with many troubles and trials. But, mind you, God has also given me many happy little things. So, along with the cup of tea, whether strong or flavorless, I have a wealth of experience to share! And people will never know if I don't tell them what my life was all about. I need to communicate to help other pilgrims on the way or to encourage those who have fallen into a pit of their own making so they can know that the God we serve is reliable, faithful, and always there for us.

I must tell somebody what it was like to live that life with

God. He has made a difference. I should tell everybody. I shudder to think about a future without His Heaven to look forward to.

I would not eliminate, if I were able, one minute of my fifty-five year journey with Paul—the good stuff, the better stuff and the worst. I have learned at the feet of my Master. Learned to keep on going and hang on to His hand.

Every day, there is a new assignment, an unexpected challenge but still and always ... God!

Oh, my very dear Paul,

I have so much to tell you. Can we sit together in a corner somewhere and chat over a cup of coffee? I can't believe that you have been up in Heaven for over five years now. I still feel as though I am only half a person, but I am learning how to walk again without a limp. I think that will make you proud.

And I must admit I can hardly wait for the day when I will hear God say, "Enough! Your time on earth is finished." I don't think I will make the summa cum laude or magna cum laude list, but it will be good enough for me to hear my God say "Well done!"

Well done, good and faithful servant!
You have been faithful with a few things;
I will put you in charge of many things.
Come and share your master's happiness
(Matthew 25:21).

It's been a lonesome journey without you.

Your Miqqy

*A Personal Note
From the
Author*

Heart: Perhaps more than any other book that I have written, I needed to finish this one. I had this pounding conviction that the story of my husband, Paul, and me, our partnership, our love, and our dreams had to be told.

Sharing over fifty years together, nearing the end of our seventies, we coped with two heartaches, Melissa's mental retardation and my husband's Parkinson's disease coupled with Alzheimer's. It's a tale told from the hilltop highs to the valley lows. Only God could have injected peace or joy into this rocky set of circumstances.

I confess it's a very personal diary of how I managed in an everyday peanut-butter world, what I coped with when I couldn't bear to let the man in my life move to a nursing home. Facing each day with its unexpected ordeals, then accepting this upside-down world alone, took a practical "hold-my-hand-Lord" dependence.

But God not only gave peace and joy, He gave the healing balm of laughter. A together kind of laughter that bound Paul's and my soul together.

Paul has been up in Heaven for almost six years now. You would think it was time enough to adjust to his absence. Yet nothing seems complete without him. I miss him dreadfully. Our love story is not a story of sublime peace and serenity. We bumbled along, exploding at times, pouting at others, then wondering why the whole wide world could not see that hanging together through the tough times is God's answer to the marriage vows.

Paul was an extraordinary person. He believed in prayer, in the Bible, and in the Lord as the living and true God, whom he could love with all his heart, soul, mind, and strength. And when, with fearful steps at times, we began to build Melmark together, it was a matter of mission: of building a world much broader and deeper for our daughter Melissa and her peers.

Perhaps baby Martha and Melissa were no accident, but a calling. Paul sensed, as someone once said that "Jesus was brilliantly disguised at Melmark." For those families who looked to this man with such a tender heart of compassion for answers, Melmark was his gift, and the family of able and disabled became his family.

Now, living alone in this retirement community of senior citizens in Rexford, New York, I listen for God's voice to call me home. And, while I wait, I want my face to shine with God's goodness and love.

Miggy

Here are more Great Books from Cook to help you deal with Life's most Difficult Challenges

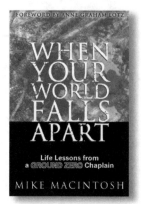

When Your World Falls Apart
Life Lessons From a Ground Zero Chaplain
(Foreword by Anne Graham Lotz)
Mike MacIntosh

One of the most vividly remembered tragedies in recent history took place on 9/11/01, but there are thousands of other disasters that never make the news. They happen to us, our family, our friends. Death, bankruptcy, divorce, terminal illness—any of these and other tragedies can leave people feeling devastated. As a member of a National Disaster Response Team, Mike was on call for the month of September 2001 and spent several weeks ministering to rescue personnel at the site of the World Trade Center disaster. While he describes some of his New York encounters, this book focuses on helping readers make it through their own devastating experiences, and on moving forward with God.

ISBN: 0-78143-889-6   ITEM #: 102067   Retail: $12.99   (Can. $21.99)
Format: PB   Size: 5 1/2 x 8 1/2   Pages: 224
Category: Christian Living   Brand: Life Journey

Power Over Panic
Answers for Anxiety
Carol M. Christensen

Not surprisingly, in a society that has become fraught with terrorism and war, anxiety disorders are on the rise. Almost everyone knows someone who is plagued by an anxiety disorder, or may themselves be the person facing this overwhelming illness. As a licensed mental health counselor and a successful Meier New Life therapist, Carol Christensen uses her skills to help people successfully identify the true source of their fear and panic. Readers learn to unlock the doors of their past that can hide and often explain compulsive behaviors. Let the healing journey begin now. You can have *Power Over Panic.*

ISBN: 0-78143-911-6   ITEM #: 102205   Retail: $14.99   (Can. $24.99)
Format: HC   Size: 5 1/2 x 8 1/2   Pages: 192   Category: Self-Help Brand: Life Journey

Gaining Through Losing
Evelyn Christenson

God can use even the most traumatic setbacks in life, such as death or divorce, to propel us forward. Beloved author Evelyn Christenson shows how the hardest of times can enrich believers.

ISBN: 0-78143-441-6   ITEM #: 99218   Retail: $11.99   (Can. $19.99)
Format: PB   Size: 5 1/2 x 8 1/2   Pages: 204   Category: Self-Help   Brand: Victor

Order in one of These Convenient Methods:
Visit your Local Christian Bookstore
Order Online: www.cookministries.com
Or Phone: 1 (800) 323-7543

It Hurts To Lose A Special Person
Amy Ross Mumford

The combination of words and photographs make this an ideal gift to unfold God's grace and love for the person suffering from the loss of a loved one.

ISBN: 0-89636-093-8 ITEM #: 54049
Retail: $5.99 (Can. $9.99)
Format: PB   Size: 5 5/8 x 8 1/4   Pages: 24
Category: Self Help Brand: Victor

Dare to Trust, Dare to Hope Again
Living With Losses of the Heart
Kari West

There is life after loss—that is the heartfelt message of this book for women who have suffered loss. Practical and inspirational meditations remind readers that God understands their loss and encourages emotional and spiritual growth during the grieving process. Motivates readers to not lose hope—and to dare to trust again.

ISBN: 0-78143-587-0 ITEM #: 100386   Retail: $13.99 (Can. $22.99)
Format: HC   Size: 5 1/2 x 7 1/2   Pages: 200 Category: Self-Help
Brand: Faithful Woman

You Gotta Keep Dancin'
In the midst of life's hurts, you can choose Joy!
Tim Hansel

Through this powerful account of God's working in the midst of physical and emotional suffering, the reader will better understand that joy is a choice in and through pain. .

ISBN: 1-56476-744-2 ITEM #: 59204   Retail: $9.99 (Can. $16.99)
Format: PB   Size: 5 1/2 x 781/2   Pages: 160 Brand: Victor

Order in one of These Convenient Methods:
Visit your Local Christian Bookstore
Order Online: www.cookministries.com
Or Phone: 1 (800) 323-7543